RIGHTS FROM WRONGS

RIGHTS
FROM WRONGS

A Secular Theory of the
Origins of Rights

ALAN DERSHOWITZ

A Member of the Perseus Books Group
New York

Books published by Basic Books are available at special discounts for
bulk purchases in the United States by corporations, institutions, and
other organizations. For more information, please contact the Special
Markets Department at the Perseus Books Group, 11 Cambridge
Center, Cambridge MA 02142, or call (617) 252–5298 or (800)
255–1514, or e-mail special.markets@perseusbooks.com.

Library of Congress Cataloging-in-Publication Data
Dershowitz, Alan M.
    Rights from wrongs / Alan Dershowitz.
        p.   cm.
    Includes bibliographical references and index.
    ISBN 0-465-01713-4 (hardcover : alk. paper)
    1. Human rights.   2. Civil rights.   I. Title.
JC571.D3985   2005
323—dc22

                                                        2004020006

04 05 06 / 10 9 8 7 6 5 4 3 2 1

This book is respectfully dedicated to the countless victims of terrible human wrongs—wrongs that have been the source of human rights. May these rights help to prevent the recurrence of these and other wrongs.

CONTENTS

ACKNOWLEDGMENTS

Because *Rights from Wrongs* represents a summary of my life's work—my thinking, teaching, writing and advocacy over nearly half a century—it owes much to many colleagues, students, friends and family. Special thanks to my current research staff: Alex Blenkinsopp for his assistance on footnotes and endnotes and his perceptive comments on the text; Eric Citron, Ayelet Weiss, Sivan Zaitchik and Matthew Stein for their research; Jane Wagner for her all around help in producing the manuscript. A word of appreciation to my editor Bill Frucht for his brilliant improvements, my agent Helen Rees and all the professionals at Basic Books, especially David Shoemaker. My thanks as well to my Martha's Vineyard friends for their creative kibitzing. As usual, my deepest gratitude and love to family members who encouraged and gently criticized me.

Finally, my appreciation to all those who have participated in the eternal struggle for rights.

Where Do Rights Come From?[1]

IN A WORLD full of wrongs, rights have never been so important. We tend to take our rights for granted until they are endangered, and we appreciate them most when we are at risk of losing them. Today there are powerful forces that pose grave dangers to rights that we have long taken for granted. At the same time, many defenders of rights insist that we accept the case for them essentially on faith. The debate has become polemical, with one side arguing that the new reality of global terrorism changes everything, while the other argues that it changes nothing. A more nuanced discussion is needed to strike the appropriate and ever-changing balance between security and liberty. Any such discussion must include the question: Where do rights come from? The answer to this question is important because the source of our rights determines their status, as well as their content.

Our founding document of liberty, the Declaration of Independence, pointed to God as the source of our rights. Among the "truths" that were regarded by our founding fathers as "self-evident" was the proposition that certain rights were "unalienable" because their source was neither government nor popular acceptance, but the endowment of the "Creator." What God gives, no human can take away. As the young Alexander Hamilton insisted on the eve of the American Revolution: "The sacred rights of mankind are not to be rummaged for among old parchments or musty records. . . . They are written, as with a sunbeam, in the whole *volume* of human nature by the hand of the divinity itself and can never be erased or obscured by mortal power."[2] Nor is this an anachronistic view. President George W. Bush put it this way in 2002: "We need common-sense judges who understand our rights were derived from God."[3]

If only it were that simple! If only it were true that a God, in whom everyone believed, had come down from the heavens and given the entire world an unambiguous list of the rights with which He endowed us. How much easier it would be to defend these sacred rights from alienation by mere mortals. Alas, the claim that rights were written down by the hand of the divinity is one of those founding myths to which we desperately cling, along with the giving of the Tablets to Moses on Sinai, the dictation of the Koran to Muhammad, and the discovery of the Gold Plates by Joseph Smith.

To the extent the divine source and unalienability of our rights are purported to be factual, history has proved our founding fathers plainly wrong: Every right has in fact been alienated by governments since the beginning of time. Within a generation of the establishment of our nation, the founding fathers rescinded virtually every right they had previously declared unalienable. John Adams, one of the drafters of the Declaration of Independence, alienated the right to speak freely and express dissenting views when, as president, he enforced the Alien and Sedition Acts against his political opponents—with Hamilton's strong support.[4] (Perhaps Hamilton's God had not given "sacred rights" to Jeffersonians!) Another of the drafters, Thomas Jefferson, alienated the most basic of rights—to the equal protection of the laws, based on the "truth" that "all men are created equal"—when he helped to write (and strengthen) Virginia's "Slave Code," just a few years after drafting the Declaration of Independence. The revised Code denied Negro slaves the right to liberty and to the pursuit of happiness by punishing attempted escape with "outlawry" or death. Jefferson personally suspected that "the blacks . . . are inferior to the whites in the endowments of body and mind." In other words, they were endowed by their creator not with equality but with inferiority.

There is no right that has not been suspended or trampled during times of crisis and war, even by our greatest presidents. Washington was a strong supporter of the Alien and Sedition Acts. Lincoln suspended the writ of habeas corpus. Wilson authorized the "Palmer raids," in which his attorney general seized, arrested, and imprisoned thousands of suspected radicals in violation of their rights. Roosevelt ordered the detention of more than 100,000 Americans of Japanese descent without even a semblance of due process. He also convened a military tribunal to try—without a jury—an American citizen caught spying for Germany in the United States. And Presidents Truman and Eisenhower, despite their personal dislike of Senator Joseph McCarthy, alienated the rights of political dissent during the Cold War by enforcing the persecution of Communists, former Communists, and those suspected of leftist sympathies.

These precedents and others have been cited by President George W. Bush, his attorney general, and some judges to justify the alienation of some of our most important rights (perhaps Bush's God did not bestow these rights on American citizens suspected of terrorism or foreigners detained at Guantanamo, Cuba). The difference is that in the past, the alienations were temporary, lasting only as long as the war or emergency. But the "war" against terrorism is, by its nature, unending. There will be no formal surrender by our current enemies. There will be no peace treaty, parades, or victory days. Whatever alienations of our fundamental rights are authorized by the courts today will endure for generations. Alienation may well become the norm.

If we most appreciate our rights when they are at risk, then the time has come to show appreciation and to struggle for the preser-

vation of our most important rights. I wish I could make an intellectually satisfying argument for the divine source of rights, as our
founding fathers tried to do. Tactically that would be the strongest
argument, especially in America where many hold a strong belief in
an intervening God. But I cannot offer this argument, because I do
not believe in concepts like divine hands, unalienability, or self-
evident truths. I am a pragmatist, a utilitarian, an empiricist, a
secularist, and (God forgive me!) a moral relativist.* I reject absolutes (except that my rejection of absolutes is itself fairly absolute; as George Bernard Shaw cynically quipped: "The golden
rule is that there are no golden rules").

There is no right that is not, in my view, immune from some alienation—or balancing—under certain extreme circumstances. Neverthe-
less, I believe strongly in the concept of rights, and in certain specific
rights such as those of equality, due process, freedom of conscience and
expression, democratic participation, life, and liberty. I have devoted my
life to trying to expand these and other rights and to trying to prevent
their alienation. Though I accept the reality that rights can, in fact, diminish in extreme circumstances, the mere possibility that these circumstances may occur should not determine the content of rights during the merely difficult times that challenge every society. It is one of the
important functions of rights to prevent (or slow down) popular
wrongs during difficult times. Extremes should be regarded not as the
norm but as the exceptions. The slippery slope is not an argument
against ever contracting any rights, merely a caution against their too-
easy alienation.

It is precisely because I reject absolutes and divine endowments that I feel it is so important to make the pragmatic,

---

*I'm a moral relativist only in the sense that, explained later on in this book, although
I believe strongly in certain rights and in certain moral principles, I recognize that in
truly extraordinary situations these rights and principles may have to be balanced
against the imperative of survival.

human-centered, relativistic case for rights. That is what I try to do in this short book, beginning with the most basic question of all: Where do rights come from? Or, put more concretely: What are the sources of our rights?

This question is crucial because in the absence of an authoritative source of rights, such as God or nature, it is easy to argue that man-made rights must take a backseat to the preferences or perceived needs of the majority in a democracy. Unless there is a compelling source of rights that trumps majoritarian preferences, the default position in a democracy should be a vote of the majority. Imagine a new democracy being formed on a distant island (or planet). Everyone agrees to begin with the principle of one adult person, one vote. Someone asks, "What about the rights of minorities?" It would then be fair to ask, "Where will these rights come from? What exactly are they? And why should they trump the votes of the majority?"

The first classic answer is that rights come from a source *external* to law itself, such as nature, God, human instinct, or some other objective reality. This theory (or, more precisely, set of theories) is generally called natural law. Our Declaration of Independence explicitly cited natural law—"The laws of Nature and of Nature's God"—as the primary source of the colonists' right to separate from Great Britain.* The second classic answer is that rights are *internal* to law—that they are granted by the law itself. This is generally called positive law.

In this book I challenge the approach to rights taken by both classic natural law and classic legal positivism. I propose a third way—an experiential approach based on nurture rather than na-

---

*It had little choice, since revolution is an extra-legal remedy that cannot be justified by reference to existing "positive" law. See Chapter 6, *infra*. The Declaration also relied on experience, citing the wrongs done to the colonists by the king. In 1689, the English Declaration of Rights had invoked the "known law and statutes" of Great Britain as a source of rights, but those very laws were being used, nearly a century later, to inflict grievous wrongs on the American colonists.

ture. This approach builds a theory of rights from the bottom up, not from the top down. It constructs this theory by examining the history of injustices, inducing certain experiential lessons, and advocating rights based on those lessons. I therefore come down squarely on the side of nurture, rather than nature, as the primary source of our rights. I would prefer the term "nurtural rights" over "natural rights" if it were more pleasing to the ear.

The great fifteenth-century Jewish commentator Isaac Abravanel once observed that "experience is more forceful than logic." I would put it a bit differently: Neither logic nor experience alone is sufficient. Without a basis in experience, logic is hollow and directionless, but without logic, experience is omni-directional and subject to varying implications. Good logic must be used to derive appropriate lessons from bad experiences.[5]

The major new insight offered by my theory of rights is that it is not necessary to have a conception of the "perfect," the "best," or even the "good" society in order to decide whether rights in general, or certain rights in particular, will serve the ends of a given society. I reject Aristotle's argument that we cannot define rights without first determining "the nature of the most desirable way of life." It is enough to have a conception—or a consensus—about the very bad society, and about the wrongs that made it so. Based on this experience with wrongs, rights can be designed to prevent (or at least slow down) the recurrence of such wrongs.

There is a real advantage in building a system of rights on acknowledged wrongs rather than on idealized perfection. We will never achieve consensus over what constitutes the best, or even good society. For example, Americans will never agree on whether a pure meritocracy is better than a society based on narrowing the gaps between economic, racial, and other groups. We will not agree about whether we would be a better society if more of us went to church and based our actions on faith, or if we were to live lives based more on reason and science.[6] We will never agree on the perfect balance between today's economic needs and tomorrow's environmental problems. Nor is there consensus regarding whether it is better for the planet to be hermetically divided into nation-states or to move closer to a one-world government.

But I would bet there is widespread agreement that we never want to see a recurrence of the Holocaust, the Stalinist mass murders, the Cambodian and Rwandan genocides, slavery, lynchings, the Inquisition, or the detention of more than 100,000 Japanese Americans.[7] Most reasonable people regard terrorism directed against civilians as unjust, especially after the attacks on 9/11 and the killings in Bali and Madrid. While there is no complete consensus regarding the lessons to be drawn from this awful history, our collective experiences with injustice constitute a fruitful foundation on which to build a theory of rights.*

It is more realistic to try to build a theory of rights on the agreed-upon wrongs of the past that we want to avoid repeating, than to try to build a theory of rights on idealized conceptions of the perfect society about which we will never agree. Moreover, a theory of rights as an experiential reaction to wrongs is more empirical, observable, and debatable, and less dependent on unprovable faith, metaphor, and myth, than theories premised on sources external to human experience. At bottom, therefore, my theory of rights is more democratic and less elitist than divine or natural law theories. It is also more truthful and honest, because rights are not facts of nature, like Newton's Laws, waiting somewhere "out there"

---

*My approach does not require unanimous or even near-unanimous acceptance of these or any other events as perfect injustice. For example, I recently encountered an eminent professor who actually tried to defend the Crusades. It quickly became apparent that he was abysmally ignorant of the facts concerning the mass slaughter of Jews, Muslims, and heathens, including thousands of babies and children. Thus, I can state my view more conditionally: For those who wish to try to prevent a recurrence of events like these, the entrenchment of certain rights will prove useful.

to be discovered, deduced, or intuited. All theories of natural or divine rights are legal fictions created by human beings to satisfy the perceived need for an external and eternal source of rights to check the wrongs produced by human nature and positive law. They are sometimes benevolent fictions, but they are fictions nonetheless, and no amount of need can convert them into fact. Moreover, the fictions of natural and divine rights may be used for malevolent as well as for benevolent purposes. In any event, the reality is that rights are legal constructs devised by the minds of human beings, based on human experience, and they must be consistently defended in the court of public opinion. They must grow out of humanity's experiences with injustices.

The theory of rights presented in this book is, in a nutshell, the following:

- Rights *do not come from God,* because God does not speak to human beings in a single voice, and rights should exist even if there is no God.
- Rights *do not come from nature,* because nature is value-neutral.
- Rights *do not come from logic,* because there is little consensus about the a priori premises from which rights may be deduced.
- Rights *do not come from the law alone,* because if they did, there would be no basis on which to judge a given legal system.
- Rights *come from human experience,* particularly experience with injustice. We learn from the mistakes of history that a rights-based system and certain fundamental rights—such as freedom of expression, freedom of and from religion, equal protection of the laws, due process, and participatory democracy—are essential to avoid repetition of the grievous injustices of the past. Working from the bottom up, from a dystopian view of our experiences with injustice, rather than

from the top down, from a utopian theory of perfect justice, we build rights on a foundation of trial, error, and our uniquely human ability to learn from our mistakes in order to avoid replicating them.*

- In a word, *rights* come from *wrongs.*

In this book, I elaborate this experiential approach to "nurtural" rights and try to make a persuasive case for rights in a world so full of wrongs. I use these wrongs as the building blocks for rights. I show that rights have not been eternal, but rather have varied over place and time. Nor have rights evolved at a constant pace. Instead, like evolution itself, rights have burgeoned episodically over history, in reaction to the most grievous of wrongs. As human beings have recognized the wrongs of such institutions as slavery, genocide, and religious oppression, they have constructed new rights to prevent the recurrence of old wrongs. It is no accident that the most important rights have often burgeoned in the immediate aftermath of the most horrendous wrongs.

Since I do not believe that rights exist outside of human experience—they are not God-given, natural, or eternal—I can do no more than advocate them. I have always believed that the best defense of rights is an active and persistent advocacy rather than a passive recourse to "higher authority." Every day poses new challenges to entrenched ideologies and new opportunities to advocate rights.

The most recent of these challenges arises from the threat of terrorism, especially religiously inspired global terrorism combined with the easy availability of weapons of mass destruction. Such terrorism not only denies its direct victims the most basic of liberties

---

*This ability to derive lessons from mistakes, though limited to humans (at least for long-term lessons), has certainly not always been taken advantage of by our species. We often repeat the mistakes of the past and suffer the consequences. See George Santayana, *The Life of Reason: Reason in Common Sense* (New York: Dover, 1980), p. 284.

but also provides governments with excuses for curtailing the rights of those suspected of complicity with terrorism, as well as of other individuals and groups. This new experience with terrorism should inform our approach to rights in the future. Yet there are some who believe that since rights are immutable and unalienable, their content should remain stagnant, unaffected by ongoing experience.* In this book, I argue against both extremes and advocate an ever-changing approach to rights as checks on abuses and as protection against ever-changing wrongs. Throughout, I will test my approach to rights by applying it to the contemporary wrongs we are facing, including terrorism itself, as well as the exploitation by governments of the fear of terrorism to justify the too easy alienation of our rights.

If rights can expand based on changing experiences, so too can they contract. The virtue of a static theory of rights is that it never justifies contraction. The vice of a static approach is that it never allows for the expansion of rights to confront growing wrongs, or the adaptation of old rights to new wrongs. It is like a long-term fixed mortgage that neither raises nor lowers your payments in response to changing interest rates.

Supreme Court Justice Antonin Scalia insists that the Constitution and the rights it contains are "dead"; that the Bill of Rights means precisely "what it meant when it was adopted." He argues that this mode of interpretation makes our rights more "enduring."[8] Those who argue for "evolving" rights, such as the late Justice William J. Brennan, condemn Scalia's approach as imposing the dead hands of our forefathers on the living law—what might

---

*Some liberals argue against a stagnant view of rights and in favor of an ever-expanding conception of rights based on changing circumstances. But these same liberals are the first to argue against any contraction of, or limitation on, rights based on changing circumstances. Yet any intellectually coherent argument for a dynamic conception of rights must include the possibility of occasionally contracting rights. See this book's Conclusion, *infra*. The one-way ratchet is a metaphor, not an argument.

be called "necrocracy." But despite the metaphor of "evolving" rights, the reality is that changes in the law do not always move in one direction.

The challenge of my approach is to persuade the citizenry that experience teaches us that it is generally preferable to change certain fundamental rights in the direction of expansion and adaptation rather than contraction or inertia. But there are no guarantees. A dynamic approach is a powerful sword, but it most certainly cuts both ways.

I *The Sources of Rights*

CHAPTER 1

What Are Rights?

T HE WORD *RIGHTS** is of relatively recent origin, although the ideas embodied in it trace their roots to biblical times.[1] Nor is it free of ambiguities, multiple meanings, and deliberate misuses.** The dictionary definition of a right includes the following:

> Something that is due to a person by just claim, legal guarantee, or moral principle. . . . A power, privilege, or immunity secured to a person by law. . . . A legally enforceable claim that another will do or will not do a given act; a recognized and protected interest, the violation of which is a wrong.

---

*The word *rights* has sometimes been used as a justification for power by monarchs or by the state, as in the "divine right" of kings, or "the government has the right to collect taxes." Thomas Hobbes, in *The Leviathan,* included the "right" of the sovereign to rule as well as to censor dangerous speech. This is, in my view, a confusion of "right" with legitimate "power."

Often the word right is used in relation to disputes between or among individuals alone, without the government being directly involved, as in "your right to swing your fist ends at the tip of my nose," or "I have a right to privacy that no newspaper should be allowed to violate." This is a more complex usage, because the government plays an important role in regulating the actions of individuals and in resolving disputes between them. Thus, if a lawsuit is brought by an aggrieved individual against a private newspaper, that lawsuit must be resolved by the state through its judicial machinery. In court, the individual will invoke some right of privacy that might be protected by law, and the private newspaper will invoke its First Amendment right to

In this book I deal only with the rights of individuals in relation to government—rights that impose restrictions on the power of government to act against individuals, even if a majority of its citizens demand such action. This is the conception of rights embodied in the U.S. Constitution, whose Bill of Rights begins, "Congress shall make no law . . ." Such negative rights include the rights not to be censored by government, not to be compelled to incriminate oneself, and not to be subjected to cruel and unusual punishment. These classic "negative" rights are to be contrasted with more recently minted "positive" rights, such as the right to a free education, to health care, or to a job. I will argue for a conception of rights that consists of restrictions on the power of government to deprive anyone of those basic liberties that experience has shown are essential to prevent the recurrence of acknowledged wrongs.

Rights, thus understood, are quintessentially undemocratic, since they constrain the state from enforcing certain majoritarian preferences. If the claim of the aggrieved individual is recognized as

---

freedom of the press. A decision to make the newspaper pay compensation to the individual would constitute governmental compulsion—state action.

The classic definition of an individual right vis-à-vis government is a denial of a governmental power—a *negative* right. In recent times, the concept of *positive* rights has received attention. These rights impose affirmative *obligations* on government to act in certain ways. The right to education, health care, work, etc., are among these claimed positive rights. Then there are some rights that may involve both positive and negative aspects. These include environmental rights—the right *not* to have trees cut down or rivers polluted, but also the right *to* compel the government to take certain environmentally protective actions.

Finally, there are so-called "human rights" that transcend particular states and apply to all governments. Some of these are positive rights defined by treaty, while others purport to be natural or customary rights.

**Various modifiers other than *individual* are often placed before the word *right*. These include *human, civil, natural, inherent, divine* (or *God-given*), *inalienable* (or *unalienable*). Subtle differences are sometimes conveyed by these modifiers. Another distinction is between "negative rights" and "positive rights." More about that later.

a right, it will generally trump the will of the majority—at least the current majority. Rights are a powerful trump over mere "interests" or "preferences."*

Why then are rights accorded a special status in comparison with strongly held preferences? Why should rights trump the will of the majority? From where do these checks on majoritarian power emanate—from God or human beings, nature or nurture? Do they exist outside of the law, or are they merely creations of the law? Are they inherent and inalienable? Or are they merely the majority's self-imposed and repealable check on itself? Who should be empowered to enforce rights against governments and majorities? Are rights absolute, or must they be balanced against other considerations? What if rights clash? Who decides which one should prevail? Do rights change over time—for example, during emergencies—or are they eternal and universal? Do they vary from place to place—for example, among different cultures—or do they transcend such differences?

Of all these questions, the most challenging, both theoretically and practically, is "Where do rights come from?" The source of rights determines their status. If rights come from God, then they are truly "unalienable," as our Declaration of Independence asserted and Alexander Hamilton reiterated. If they derive from nature, then they are as immutable as the natural laws of physics and astronomy. (In English, the word *law* is used to describe both man-made rules of conduct and the formulas that describe nature. These very differ-

---

*Friedrich Hayek has observed that "only a demagogue can represent as 'anti-democratic' the limitations which long-term decisions and the general principles held by the people impose upon the power of temporary majorities." Hayek, *The Constitution of Liberty* (Chicago: University of Chicago Press, 1960) at p. 181, quoted in John Hart Ely, *Democracy and Distrust* (Cambridge, Mass.: Harvard University Press, 1980) at p. 63. The conflict Hayek poses is a *temporal* one, among democratic decisions over time. Moreover, the "general principles" he cites often mask political or ideological preferences, as they did in Hayek's case.

ent meanings have contributed to some of the confusion regarding "natural law.") But if rights are solely the product of human law-making—if they are inventions rather than discoveries—then they are subject to modification, even abrogation, by the same source that devised them in the first place. Moreover, if rights come from God or nature, how can we ever know if a particular right exists? Neither God nor nature speaks directly to us. Even the oracle at Delphi spoke more clearly than the God of nature. Did God bestow on us the right to bear arms? Has nature given us the right to own pets? The seventeenth-century philosopher Thomas Hobbes defined natural laws as "those which have been laws from all eternity," and presumably in all places. But there are no such laws, and certainly no such rights that have transcended time and place. Positive rights are far easier to discern, since they appear in law books accessible to all. Accordingly, a great deal turns on where rights come from.

Sometimes we use the word *right* descriptively, simply as a statement that the right exists, as in "the Constitution gives me a right not to be censored by the government." This is the traditional legal positivist definition of *right*—a claim grounded in enacted law.* The right may be statutory, common law, constitutional, or based on other accepted sources of authority such as a treaty, convention, or contract.[2] A descriptive right need not, however, have its source in positive law. Jefferson and Hamilton did not say that we *should* have certain natural rights, but that we *did* have those rights, endowed to

---

*According to the *Dictionary of Modern Legal Usage*, "Positive law, referring primarily to statutes and regulations, might be defined as coercively implemented law laid down within a particular community by political superiors, to govern members of the community as distinct from moral law or law existing in an ideal community or in some nonpolitical community." *Dictionary of Modern Legal Usage*, 2nd ed. (New York: Oxford University Press, 1995), p. 672.

More simply, it may be defined as "law actually and specifically enacted or adopted by proper authority for the government of an organized jural society." *Black's Law Dictionary*, 6th ed. (St. Paul, Minn.: West Publishing, 1990), p. 1162.

us by our creator. They explicitly asserted this as a self-evident "is," not an "ought."

Other times, *right* is used prescriptively, as in "I should have the right to do anything I want unless it hurts somebody else." This is John Stuart Mill's prescription for what ought to be a universal right. This claim of right has been put colloquially as "Your right to swing your fist ends at the tip of my nose," or more relevantly, "Your right to puff tobacco smoke ends at the entrance to my nostrils." But unless the right has been codified, it lacks the status of positive law. As Oliver Wendell Holmes Jr. once quipped about a claim of right grounded in the philosophy of a writer popular in his day: "The Fourteenth Amendment does not enact Mr. Herbert Spencer's Social Statics."[3]

Often there is confusion as to whether a claim of right is descriptive or prescriptive, since not everybody knows the actual content of the law—positive or natural—but nearly everybody has opinions about his or her rights.

While legal positivism grounds all law—and thus all rights—in humanly enacted rules, natural law grounds the content of rights in external sources such as God, nature, reason, or some notion of objective reality. While they differ about the sources, natural-law theorists generally agree that there are sources outside the positively enacted human laws that do or should determine the content of rights. In other words, natural law posits that we don't just make it up as we go along—that something beyond human invention determines the content of morality, law, and rights.[4] It is our job, as human beings, simply to find this something. All laws and rights are a function of this discovery process. Sir William Blackstone, whose *Commentaries on the Laws of England* have had enormous influence on Anglo-American jurisprudence, asserted that human laws may not contradict God's laws, and if they do, they have no validity. Hamilton insisted that the same would be true of rights. If a right comes from God's law, then it must supersede human law or authority. The problem is how to discern God's law. For biblical fundamentalists (not unlike constitutional "fundamentalists") the task appears deceptively simple: Look to the literal words (and original intent) of the lawgiver. But the words attributed to God are riddled with ambiguity.

Advocates of natural law often find positive law in conflict with it. For example, the decisions of the United States Supreme Court recognizing a woman's right to choose abortion are seen by many as in violation of the fetus's natural right to life. Some natural-law proponents take the position that although the Supreme Court's decisions have the status of positive law under our constitutional system, they are not really "the law" as mandated by God, nature, or reason and hence should not be followed by just people. As my colleague Lloyd Weinreb put it: Natural law asserts "that a rule of positive law that fails to conform to overriding, fully general moral principles, and is for that reason not obligatory, is not truly law at all."[5] Others say that the positive law should be followed—for either prudential or democratic reasons—but that efforts should persist to bring it in line with natural law. In condemning human embryo cell research, the Vatican recently declared it "a gravely immoral, and thus gravely illicit act,"[6] even if it is authorized by the positive law of the time and place. The same is true of gay marriage. A bishop recently characterized as "presumptuous" any attempt by a mere court to alter the definition of a "natural" and "sacramental" institution like marriage by granting gays the right to marry.

Whatever the source or sources of rights, most people see rights as something special, to be respected and not to be treated lightly. At the very least, a right must be different from a mere preference or interest. It should be something more enduring, more entrenched—something that those in positions of authority should not be able to take away, at least not without a compelling reason. Even in a democracy, the majority should not be empowered to trample the rights of minorities. A fundamental right should be harder to change than a mere legislative preference. The process of adaptation must be deliberate. The reasons justifying change should be weighty, institutional, and long term. But as the very human framers of our Constitution understood, there must be some mechanism—however cumbersome and difficult—to change positive-law rights. Hence, the amending process.

For those who believe that God is the source of all rights, they take on an even more immutable status as sacred. For those, like me, who believe that human beings design—invent—rights to prevent the recurrence of wrongs, there is a special obligation to advocate and encourage others to accept the centrality of rights in democratic societies. We have a heavier burden of persuasion, which I willingly undertake. I begin by attacking the claim that rights come from God or nature.

CHAPTER 2

Is God the Source of Rights?

THE FIRST CLAIMED external source of natural rights is God. But if rights were written by "the hand of the divinity," and if there is only one God, then the content of rights would be consistent over time and place. Yet experience shows that nothing could be further from the truth. The divine rights of one time and place have repeatedly been recognized as the human wrongs of different times and places. For example, the right to own slaves—even the right to *be* a slave—was said to come from God's Bible. Experience has demonstrated that natural rights allegedly written by the hand of the divinity can be forged by the devil, as well as by conservatives and liberals. As the British philosopher H. L. A. Hart put it: "Like a harlot, natural law is at the disposal of everyone. The ideology does not exist that cannot be defended by an appeal to the law of nature."[1]

The same can be said of divine rights: God's ambiguous words can be cited for any ideology. Those God-given rights that President Bush wants his judicial appointees to enforce (such as the right of the fetus not to be aborted, the right of public school children to pray in class, and the right of heterosexual married couples not to have their sacred institution compromised by homosexual marriage) are quite different from the God-given rights that religious liberals want to see enforced (such as the right of a woman to choose abortion, the right of public school children to be free from religious coercion, and the right of gays to marry).* Heavenly sourced rights—whether espoused by conservatives or liberals—tend to coincide with the earthly political views of those who claim God's imprimatur.

Whether consciously or not, those who purport to speak in the name of God generally use natural rights as a cover for partisan, religious, or personal agendas. For example, in 1873 the Supreme Court, in denying a woman the right to be admitted to the bar, relied on a divine concept of natural law: "God designed the sexes to occupy different spheres of action," and "It belonged to men to apply and execute the law." Women's divinely assigned role was in the "domestic sphere." Beyond "the divine ordinance" and "the law of The Creator," it is "in the nature of *things*" that women must stay home. What "things" the High Court never tells us.

God's law has been the source of justification for genocidal crusades, inquisitions, slavery, serfdom, monarchy, anti-Semitism, anti-Catholicism, bigotry against Muslims, genocide against Native Americans, homophobia, terrorism, and many other wrongs. God's law has also been cited in opposition to these evils. Today God is invoked both in support of terrorism and in justification of the war against terrorism. President Bush has told us that God, whose rights he wants his judges to enforce, wanted him to "be president" and that God personally spoke to him after September 11, 2001. Bush has claimed that "God told me to strike at al-Qaida." And lest there be any doubt about the divine provenance of the war in Iraq: "He [God] instructed me [Bush] to strike at

---

*Martin Luther King Jr. firmly believed that the liberal rights for which he fought were God-given. In his 1963 letter from Birmingham jail, King wrote, "We [Negroes] have waited for more than 340 years for our constitutional and God-given rights." He later wrote that "A just law is a man-made code that squares with the moral law or the law of God. An unjust law is a code that is out of harmony with the moral law."

Saddam, which I did."[2] Osama bin Laden claims that he too was acting under God's orders:

> The U.S. knows that I have attacked it, by the grace of God, for more than ten years now. The U.S. alleges that I am fully responsible for the killing of its soldiers in Somalia. God knows that we have been pleased at the killing of American soldiers. This was achieved by the grace of God and the efforts of the mujahedin from among the Somali brothers and other Arab mujahedin . . . America has been trying ever since to tighten its economic blockade against us and to arrest me. It has failed. This blockade does not hurt much. We expect to be rewarded by God. . . . Hostility toward America is a religious duty, and we hope to be rewarded for it by God.[3]

Earlier, bin Laden had issued a religious fatwa in which he declared, "We—with God's help—call on every Muslim who believes in God and wishes to be rewarded to comply with God's order to kill the Americans and plunder their money wherever and whenever they find it."[4] He also claimed a "religious obligation" to acquire weapons of mass destruction. God-talk only encourages the kind of theological warfare that has plagued our world and now threatens our very existence.[5]

Contemporary apologists for divine law argue that some past claims—especially those of which they disapprove—were misreadings or misapplications of God's true will. But how can we be sure that today's "correct" reading will not be subject to tomorrow's correction? The history of divine law is a history of repeated corrections of yesterday's lethal misreadings and misapplications. To be an advocate of divine law is constantly to have to say you're sorry for the mistakes of your predecessors, as your successors will inevitably have to apologize for the mistakes you are now making when you claim to know God's true intentions. In 2002 the Catholic Church finally decided it was theologically improper to try to convert the Jews. Whoops! Sorry for all those inquisitions, crusades, and autos-da-fé. Previous popes were wrong—infallible perhaps, but wrong.

Contemporary proponents of an exclusively positive law approach also have much for which to apologize with regard to the mistakes of prior positivists, such as the Nazis. (I will get to these in due course.) But at least those mistakes are conceded to be entirely human, and to err is human, but to be divine is never to err—or to have to apologize. It insults God to believe that it was He who mandated eternal inequality for women, execution for gays, slavery, animal sacrifice, and the scores of immoral laws of the Bible, the Koran, and other books purported to be speaking in God's name. Humans falsely speaking in God's name are to blame for these immoralities, just as humans must be credited with the hundreds of morally elevating laws in these holy books. And it is humans who must continue to change law and morality so as to remain more elevated than the animals, who indeed cannot rise above the law of nature.

In a diverse world where many claim to know God's will, and where there is consensus about neither its content nor the methodology for discerning it,[6] God should not be invoked as the source of our political rights. In the 2000 U.S. presidential election, Senator Joseph Lieberman repeatedly invoked God as the source of American rights, citing our Declaration of Independence and even going so far as to assert that morality cannot be "maintained without religion"—a demonstrably false and insulting assertion.[7] In the current debate over gay marriage, a minister announced from the steps of the Capitol that this is a battle between gays and God, and that he represents God. And a candidate for the United States Senate—Alan Keyes—proclaimed that a victory for him would be a "victory . . . for God."[8]

The traditional case for divine rights is an uncomfortable one to make in a religiously and philosophically diverse democracy, since the claimed external source for such natural rights seems ill-suited to such a society. In any event, for the millions of good and moral people who do not believe in God, or in an intervening God, or who are agnostic about these matters, or who believe in a separation between religion and government—there must be other sources of law and rights. It surely cannot be the case that only those who believe in a God who directs the destiny of humankind can have a theory of rights. Many of those who first articulated our rights did not believe in such a God.[9] In our pluralistic society, all citizens should be entitled to participate in the conversation about rights without any religious litmus test. Rights are too important to be left only to theological discourse. As I will show, rights should be recognized even in the absence of an intervening God.

Is Nature the Source of Rights?

T HE SECOND TRADITIONAL source of natural rights is that they derive somehow from the laws of the physical universe or the nature of human beings. There are several variations on this general theme. The first is closely related to the argument discussed in the previous chapter, namely, that God is the source of all rights. If God created the laws of the universe and of human nature, then it would follow logically that rights derive from nature and from "nature's God." Alexander Pope offered this perspective in a poem entitled "An Essay on Man: Epistle I":

All are but parts of one stupendous whole,
Whose body Nature is, and God the soul; . . .
All Nature is but art, unknown to thee;
All chance, direction, which thou canst not see;
All discord, harmony not understood;
All partial evil, universal good:
And, spite of pride, in erring reason's spite,
One truth is clear, whatever is, is right.

If God is perfect (or right) and if God created nature, it would follow that "whatever is, is right." If what "is" does not appear "right," that is because we "canst not see" or understand God's ways. For those

who believe that nature is "the image of God," as did Blaise Pascal, or the "art of God," as did Dante,[1] the conclusion that nature is good is little more than a theological tautology that follows from the premise that God is good and omnipotent. But experience makes this tautology difficult to accept, because much of what "is" cannot, by any stretch of language or logic, be deemed "right." The rules that govern the physical universe are morally neutral—that is, they are neither "right" nor "wrong"; they simply "are." The results produced by these laws and by human nature are certainly not always "right," as anyone can observe. If we accept horrendous outcomes—suffering, death, slavery, genocide—as "right," then the word loses all human meaning. It is interesting how religious fundamentalists credit God with the beautiful or positive results of nature, but only rarely blame Him for the ugly and the negative. How frequently have we heard survivors of natural disaster credit God for saving them, and how infrequently have we heard them blame God for killing those who did not survive these very same "acts of God."*

Even for those believers who recognize that truly bad or evil results are sometimes produced by the workings of God's rules of nature, there is always the solace of the afterlife: "God has a plan," "All will be right in the end." Finally, for those who are uncertain of heavenly rewards there is always the claim, made so poetically by Pope, that "God works in mysterious ways" defying human comprehension. To this reductionistic argument, I am always tempted to reply, "I'm sorry, I *am* fully capable of understanding that the Holocaust, slavery, and the

---

*During the standoff over what to do with Elian Gonzalez, who was rescued and brought to the United States after the November 1999 Cuban-refugee-boat sinking that killed his mother, a spokesman for Elian's Miami relatives said, "The family does not feel defeated and they still have faith in God that the Supreme Court will accept the appeal in the same way God saved Elian from drowning." No mention was made of Elian's mother. People often wonder how God could have allowed bad things to happen to them, but the degree of blame for bad things rarely equals the degree of credit for good things.

genocide against Native Americans were unmitigated evils by any meaningful definition of that term." What "was" during the Holocaust was not "right," and no amount of religious sophistry can make it right. Moreover, to conclude that "whatever is, is right" constitutes an invitation to accepting wrongs as inevitable. Human beings should do everything in their power to prevent recurrence of these and other wrongs, and the first step is to recognize them as wrongs. Only then can we take steps designed to prevent their recurrence. These steps include the enactment of rights whose absence may have contributed to the facilitation of these wrongs. If "whatever is, is right," then we do not need laws or rights to improve on nature. After all, why try to change what "is right"?

George Bernard Shaw answered Alexander Pope's invitation to inaction when he wrote: "You see things; and you say, 'Why?' But I dream things that never were; and I say, 'Why not?'"

Not all religious views accept the rightness of nature, even if God is its creator. The Jewish concept of Tikun Olam—repairing the world—would seem to imply the imperfection of nature and the human obligation of improving on the natural condition of the world. According to a midrash, God needed human beings to complete the ongoing process of creation—to make nature better. The Bible commands "justice, justice shall you *pursue*," suggesting an active and never-ending quest that assumes the perfectibility of even God's nature.

Another variation on the theme of natural laws relies less directly on God and more on the nature of human beings (whether or not God endowed humans with this nature). But human beings have no singular nature. We include the best and the worst. We are creatures of accidental forces who have no preordained destiny or purpose. We must make our own destiny and determine our own purposes. To attempt to derive normative rights from descriptions—even if accurate—of human nature is to indulge in a variation on the "nat-

uralistic fallacy."* The naturalistic fallacy describes—and exposes—
the error of confusing what *is* with what *ought* to be, because it is
"logically impossible for any set of statements of the kind usually
called descriptive to entail a statement of the kind usually called
evaluative."[2] Though this rigid epistemological formulation may
overstate the lack of connection between the "is" of empiricism and
the "ought" of morality, it is certainly true that there is no necessary
correlation between what is and what ought to be in a world capable of constant improvement and increasing aspirations.

There have always been some who believe that we cannot improve upon nature. The idea that nature is inherently good—that
it contains a positive moral component or leads in a positive
moral direction—goes back a considerable time. The first-century
poet Juvenal insisted that: "Never does nature say one thing and
wisdom another," as did Augustine three hundred years later: "All
nature is good." The sixteenth-century English author John Florio
called nature "the right law." Perhaps in physics! But certainly not
in morality. Cicero believed that "whatever befalls in the course of
nature should be considered good."[3] Unless this is meant to be a
meaningless tautology, it is completely contradicted by human experience, which shows that so much that "befalls" us is demonstrably bad. Of course, for those who have lived privileged lives
and have come out on top, the "is" becomes a vindication of the
"ought" of their own lives.

---

*The "naturalistic fallacy" refers to G. E. Moore's discussion of the analytical flaw
whereby a person "is *either* confusing Good with a natural *or* metaphysical property
or holding it to be identical with such a property or making an inference *based* on
such a confusion" (emphasis added). Casmir Levy, "G. E. Moore on the Naturalistic
Fallacy," in *G. E. Moore—Essays in Retrospect*, eds. Alice Ambrose and Morris Laze-
rowitz (London: Allen and Unwin, 1970). David Hume also articulated a formulation
of the naturalistic fallacy in book III, part I, section I of his *Treatise of Human Nature*
(1739). He observed that writers proffering views of morality tend to replace "is" with
"ought" as they proceed through their arguments.

In this regard, I am reminded of one of the most immoral of religious pronouncements, attributed to King David as the author of the Psalms. In Psalm 37, David makes the following observation: "I was young and I also became old, yet I never observed a righteous person abandoned or his children wanting for bread." Only a king, isolated in his splendid palace, could fail to observe, or experience, righteous people being abandoned and their children afflicted with poverty. As the philosopher Mel Brooks had the royal character he played put it in *The History of the World Part I:* "It's good to be king." His other, more humble character—the man whose job it was to empty the royal chamber pots—might have seen the world quite differently.[4] Brooks had more insight in this regard than David.

During the era in which our Declaration of Independence was written, many scientists believed that bodies of "truth" were out there waiting to be discovered—and that once discovered, these truths were as "self-evident" as Newton's law of gravity. These transcendent and static bodies included not only physical truths but also moral truths, perhaps even legal truths. There was little dispute between science and morality (whether religiously based or not) about this conception.

Many prominent legal scholars of that age—Blackstone was among the most influential both in England and in the colonies—believed that the law was a truth to be discovered. Blackstone maintained that there are "eternal, immutable laws of good and evil, to which the creator himself in all his dispensations conforms; and which he has enabled human reason to discover, so far as they are necessary for the conduct of human actions." The American school of legal realism—beginning with Holmes and reaching its zenith in the mid-twentieth century—changed all of that. Few contemporary scholars actually believe that the law is an abstraction in the sky, rather than a human invention. "The life of the law," Holmes correctly observed, "has not been logic; it has been experience." And the implications of experience for "truth" are neither static nor self-evident. Experience, morality, legality, even truth are ever-changing, always-adapting, constantly interacting with nature and nurture.

Today, there are few reputable scientists who believe that moral or legal truths are comparable to physical or scientific truths. The entire vocabulary has changed, as we recognize that the "laws" of physics bear no relation—other than sharing a common word in *some* languages—to the "laws" of morality or the "laws" that are enacted by legislatures to govern our conduct. Most modern thinkers accept Spinoza's more skeptical view, echoed by my late friend and colleague Stephen Jay Gould, that "nature has no goal in view, and final causes are only human imaginings."[5] As Robert G. Ingersoll wrote in 1881: "We must remember that in nature there are neither rewards nor punishments—there are consequences."[6] Its rules existed before human consciousness, and they would have operated even if no human being ever appeared in the world. Nature does what it does because of factors entirely irrelevant to human morality. Nor are the wonders of nature proof of any moral component for those who believe that "the beauty, symmetry, regularity and order seen in the universe are the aspects of a blind intelligent nature."[7] As Anatole France once observed: "Nature has no principles, she furnishes us with no reason to believe that human life is to be respected. Nature, in its indifference, makes no distinction between good and evil." Even Einstein, who famously quipped that "God does not play dice with the universe," did not believe that the immutable rules of nature were directly translatable into eternal laws of human morality.

Anyone observing nature with an objective eye will see that it is morally neutral. It is full of beauty and wonder, but it thrives on violence and predation. Nature is a mother animal nursing her helpless cub and then killing another helpless animal to survive. Nature is life-giving sunshine followed by death-dealing floods. Human nature is Albert Schweitzer and Adolf Hitler; Jesus and Torquemada;

Kant and Nietzsche; Confucius and Pol Pot; Mandela and bin Laden; the early Martin Luther, who reached out to the despised, and the later Martin Luther, who advocated rounding up the Jews and making them "miserable captives" in forced-labor camps. Human nature is radical Muslims dancing in the streets at the sight of Americans jumping to their deaths from the Twin Towers—and other Muslims going to their mosques and praying for the survival of victims of terrorism. Human nature is Hamas building schools and medical centers for Islamic children and Hamas blowing up Jewish children on the way to their schools.

This is not to deny that there is a relationship between nature and morality. Any attempt to build a system of morality that completely ignores nature will fail. Nature has a vote but not a veto on questions of morality. The naturalistic fallacy has a mirror-image fallacy: namely, that moral prescriptions can totally ignore nature. We can call this the nurturalistic fallacy. Nurture alone cannot determine the content of morality or rights. Nature must be taken into account. In deciding on a sexual morality appropriate for a given society it is important to understand the nature of the sex drive. For example, efforts to deter adolescent masturbation as "unnatural" and therefore "wrong" are doomed to failure, because the nature of adolescent sexuality is more powerful than the threats of punishment for this entirely harmless—and I would add "natural"—outlet. Many Catholics are now questioning whether priestly celibacy is compatible with the natural sex drive.

But morality cannot and should not be derived directly from nature. Even if sociobiologists were to prove that men are naturally inclined to force women into sexual submission, there would be no "right" to rape. It would still be morally wrong for a society not to make every reasonable effort to hold this "natural impulse" in check, because even if it is empirically natural, it is morally wrong, as we have learned from experience. "Doing what comes naturally" may be a good song title, but it is a terrible rule of morality. Rape is horribly wrong even though the men who wrote the Bible did not think it was wrong enough to include in the Ten Commandments. They did, however, include voluntary adultery, but only if it involved a married *woman*! We can improve on the Ten Commandments, because we have much more human experience on which to base our rules than did the men who wrote the Bible, just as the authors of the Ten Commandments improved on the Code of Hammurabi and earlier laws.

In constructing a moral code or a system of rights one should not ignore the varieties of human nature, or their alleged commonalities. But neither can the diverse components of nature be translated directly into morality, legality, or rights. The complex relationship between the "is" of nature and the "ought" of morality must be mediated by human experience. The history of rights illustrates this complexity. A rights-based system is certainly not the natural human condition. If there is any natural condition, it is closer to tyranny. The history of humankind has been a history in which the norm has almost always been authoritarianism, elitism, censorship, arbitrariness, and denial of what we have come to call due process of law.[8] Dostoyevsky's Grand Inquisitor saw the surrender to tyranny as necessary to deliver human beings from "their present terrible torments of personal and free decision." He predicted that people will come to understand that "they can never be free, for they are weak, vicious, worthless and rebellious," and that in the end even the most rebellious "will become obedient."

For those, like Jean-Jacques Rousseau, who believe that "man is born free," the question arises, why then is he everywhere "in chains"? Why, as Thomas Hobbes observed, is the "life of man . . . solitary, poor, nasty, brutish, and short"? The answer is because that is closer to the natural human condition, at least descriptively, than any system based on rights. The function of rights—indeed, of law and morality—is to change that natural condition for the better: to improve upon nature, to domesticate its wild beast, and to elevate us from the terrible state of nature into a state of civilization. It is a never-ending challenge. If the advocates of rights fall asleep at the wheel for even one historical moment, there is danger that the natural human condition will rear its ugly head, as it has so many times over the millennia.

Yet from the beginning of recorded history, a relatively small number of liberty-loving individuals have struggled against the deeply ingrained human need for authority, control, domination, paternalism, and, indeed, tyranny. They have lived and died for rights. It is too early in the annals of humankind to know with any degree of certainty whether the entrenched forces of authoritarianism will once again prevail over the recurrent but episodic demands for liberty. What is certain is that the struggle for liberty—and for rights—never stays won. Consider Germany, for example, which had a long tradition of liberty, at least among its intelligentsia. It then quickly succumbed to Nazism. Among the most influential Nazi supporters were leading intellectuals, artists, lawyers, businessmen, church leaders, and doctors.

It is precisely because rights are not natural—that it is not in the nature of most human beings to value the rights of others above their own immediate interests—that we need to entrench certain basic rights, continuously advocate them, and never grow complacent about them. If rights were as natural as some claim, we could expect them to be far more popular than they have ever been among the general public. Valuing rights may be more "natural" among some elements of society than others, and it is the responsibility of the former to persuade the latter of their importance.

We need rights to offset the natural instinct of most human beings to take what they can get, with little concern for the interests of others, particularly strangers. It should not be surprising that among the first rules of religion, civility, and community are "Love your neighbor *as yourself*" and "What you would not have done *to yourself*, do not do to others." Listen to a portion of John Adams's argument in defense of the British soldiers who were accused of participating in the Boston Massacre and who claimed the right of self-defense against rock-throwing provocateurs:

> The first branch [of human duty] is self-love. [God] has implanted it there. . . . Blackstone calls it "the primary canon" in the law of nature. That precept of our Holy religion which commands us to love our neighbor as ourselves . . . enjoins that our benevolence to our fellow men, should be as real and sincere as our affections to ourselves, not that it should be as great in degree.[9]

The secular Oliver Wendell Holmes Jr. echoed Adams's religiously based views when he declared that "in the last resort a man rightly prefers his own interest to that of his neighbor."[10] This recognition of the natural selfishness of most human beings has formed the basis for much religious, economic, political, and philosophical doctrine. John Rawls's influential "original position" is a variation on this recognition of inherent selfishness. The "veil of ignorance" is designed to preclude those in the original position from acting on their selfishness, by denying them knowledge necessary to make self-serving decisions.[11] Kant believed that our first political duty is to leave the state of nature, where selfishness is the first rule of survival, and submit ourselves along with others to the rule of a reasonable and just law.[12]

These religious and philosophical approaches are striking examples of human beings recognizing the natural "is" of selfishness and aspiring to the less natural "ought" of altruism. That aspiration, I would argue, grows out of our human experience with the wrongs produced by untrammeled selfishness. This recognition is an important building block for any system of individual rights.

CHAPTER 4

Are There Other "External" Sources of Rights?

IF RIGHTS DO not come from God or from nature, where else could they come from? For traditional legal positivists, the answer is simple: from the human beings who write the laws. But what if these human beings decide that there should be no rights? Or what if they refuse to enact specific rights deemed by many to be fundamental, such as freedom of speech, equality under law, or due process? Would those rights cease to exist, or could people still claim those rights based on some authority outside of existing positive law? If rights are natural and hence universal—as are physical laws—then local positive laws cannot abridge them. The French Parliament cannot amend Newton's Laws or change pi from 3.14 to 4.

At one level, the right to be governed by the rule of law, as distinguished from the arbitrary whim of man, is itself an important foundation stone of any system of rights. In that respect, positive law does bestow an important right, even without regard to its content. But the right to be governed by the rule of law may be empty—or worse—as exemplified by the positive laws that governed slaves in the American South or Jews in Nazi Germany or dissidents in the Soviet Union.* As

---

*The Soviet Union, even under Stalin, had a wonderful Constitution that was applied by KGB-dominated courts.

Justice Robert Jackson observed, "The most odious of all oppressions are those which mask as justice."[1] Although the absence of positive laws, accessible to all, may deny a basic right, the enactment of such laws—the establishment of the rule of law—does not by itself assure rights to all, even if it does to some. If a particular rule of law—such as the slave codes and the Nuremberg laws—denies fundamental rights to a minority, can it be said that all their "rights" are eliminated by the positive law?

Questions of this kind have daunted legal philosophers for generations. In recent times, a new genre of thinkers has sought to occupy a middle ground between the metaphysics of traditional natural law and the reductionism of traditional legal positivism. Perhaps the most influential of these thinkers is Ronald Dworkin. Dworkin rejects simple legal positivism, insisting that "Plainly, any rights-based theory must presume rights that are not simply the product of deliberate legislation or explicit social custom, but are independent grounds for judging legislation and custom." Rights are, to Dworkin, "political trumps held by individuals," which necessarily exist outside of the positive law, because people have "moral rights against their governments."[2] This is not a definition of *rights*, but rather an indication of their status. Nor does it tell us where rights come from. On this important question, Dworkin is at his weakest.

Dworkin is suspicious of rights that purport to come from God: "The institution of rights against the Government is not a gift of God, or an ancient ritual, or a national sport."[3] Nor are they "to be found in natural law or locked up in some transcendental strongbox." By strongbox, Dworkin apparently means some fixed physical container, like the Dead Sea scrolls, or some metaphysical repository, such as the "brooding omnipresence in the sky." He rejects this "strongbox theory" as "nonsense." Indeed he insists on avoiding the term "natural law," because "it has, for many people, disqualifying metaphysical associations. They think that natural rights are supposed to be spectral attributes worn by primitive men like amulets, which they carry into civilization to ward off tyranny."[4]

He seems equally suspicious of "ghostly entities like collective wills, or national spirits." His "idea of individual rights . . . does not presuppose any ghostly forms."[5] Nor does he accept John Rawls's "intuitionistic" assumptions about "innate categories of morality common to all men, imprinted in their neural structure." (In support of an intuition for rights, a colleague has observed that children are always invoking their "rights" in relation to their parents. This is surely true today in America, but it was just as surely not true in the past and in other places. In fact, the observation supports the view that there is no hardwired intuition for rights and that they are more nurtural than natural. We live today in a culture of rights and kids pick up on that culture at a very early age. I know! I have a teenager![6])

Dworkin observes that the majority of citizens, even in the United States and Britain, "do not exercise the political liberties that they have, and would not count the loss of these liberties as especially grievous." He cites the psychologist Ronald Laing in support of a proposition made by Dostoyevsky's Grand Inquisitor, namely, that "a good deal of mental instability in modern societies may be traced to the demand for too much liberty rather than too little."[7] I am not sure that Dworkin is correct in predicting that Americans would accept the loss of certain rights that we passively take for granted, such as the right not to be censored by government or the right not to have our homes searched without a warrant. But his general point, that most American and British citizens do not actively exercise their rights, is probably true. Moreover history has demonstrated that most people throughout the world do not seem to possess Rawls's intuition for rights (though there may be some intuition for basic fairness, especially among those who perceive themselves as victims of unfairness).[8]

Rawls has not been alone in looking to human intuition as a source of rights. Jefferson argued that American colonists "felt their rights before they had thought through their explanation." He famously observed that if you "state a moral case to a ploughman and a professor," the ploughman "will decide it as well and often better . . . because he has not been led astray by artificial rules." I would disagree based on my experiences (though I must admit I have met very few ploughmen in my life). People may feel *their own* rights instinctively, but this is far less true for the rights of *others*, especially when they conflict with their own preferences.[9] Moreover, even if there were to be some instinct for rights, the content of such rights would differ over time, place, and experience.

Though Dworkin appears to side with me on this score and against Jefferson and Rawls, he still insists, along with traditional proponents of natural law, that rights must be "discovered" rather than invented or created. "It remains the judge's duty, even in hard cases, to discover what the rights of the parties are, not to invent new rights retrospectively."[10]

What is the difference between a discovery and an invention? Discoveries are inevitable. It is only a matter of time before someone finds or stumbles upon a place, phenomenon, or physical law that exists in nature. An argument between Jerry Seinfeld and George Costanza about their favorite explorer makes this point:

GEORGE: Magellan? You like Magellan?
JERRY: Oh, yeah. My favorite explorer. Around the world. Come on.
  Who do you like?
GEORGE: I like de Soto.
JERRY: De Soto? What did he do?
GEORGE: Discovered the Mississippi.
JERRY: Oh, like they wouldn't have found that anyway.

Discovery connotes an existing entity waiting to be found, if only we look in the right places. And Dworkin tells us where to look if we are to discover the source of our rights: He suggests that "we discover what rights people actually have by looking for arguments that would justify [certain] claims." He locates such non-positive rights within a "constructive model," which human beings build "as if a sculptor set himself to carve the animal that best fits a pile of bones he happened to find together." This man-made constructive model is to be contrasted with the kind of natural model that derives from "an objective moral reality," not created by men or societies but rather "discovered by them, as they discover laws of physics."[11] The "bones" from which Dworkin constructs his model of rights consist of principles related to the equality of human beings.[12]

Dworkin's core principle is that governments must treat all their citizens with equal concern and respect. This principle is a fundamental "postulate of political morality" to which all reasonable people must adhere. That is his discovery, but he doesn't tell us *where* he discovered it. Certainly not in the history of humankind. No objective assessment of history will show a universal postulate of equality that transcends time and place. If anything, human beings have always constructed hierarchies of inequality.

Dworkin's alleged discovery of a postulate of human equality is not something that can simply be found by looking in the right place. It is not an eternal truth as a matter of descriptive history, since elitism, hierarchy, and inequality have been the norm during most of human experience. What Dworkin correctly observes about political liberties—that most people do not seem to exercise, or care much about, them—I would argue is at least as true of equality: Few people really care whether *other* people or other groups are treated equally, so long as they themselves come out on or near the top. Even the theoretical arguments for equal treatment, hypocritical as they often are in the face of practice, are of relatively recent origin. Counterarguments against equality—certainly against some forms of equality—have been made since the beginning of time, as I will soon show. And these arguments, often based on God and nature, won the day until relatively recently. The source of rights cannot be discovered therefore "in arguments" of the kind cited by Dworkin.

I agree that human equality should be an important foundation stone for any theory of rights, but I would argue that it is an invention rather than a discovery.

A more persuasive argument for the right to equal treatment would be built on our collective negative experience with the wrongs of unequal treatment during slavery, the Holocaust, the Inquisition, and other disastrous human epochs. Experience has shown that societies that treat people unequally—that deny most of them any semblance of equality of opportunity—end up with dissatisfaction, disorder, and violence. Talented individuals who have the potential to add value to the society are denied the opportunity to make a contribution and thus feel less of a stake in the society. There seems to be an emerging consensus that some degree of equality of opportunity is essential to avoiding a bad or unjust society. There is certainly no consensus, however, about whether the perfect or good society demands equality of *outcome,* rather than of *opportunity.*[13] Decent human beings invented the counterintuitive right to equal treatment as a mechanism for avoiding recurrence of the wrongs of unequal opportunity—wrongs we now recognize to be immoral.

Regardless of whether the right to equal treatment is a discovery, as Dworkin insists, or an invention, as I believe, some other basic rights do flow logically from this egalitarian postulate—this right to equal treatment. Precisely what these derivative rights are will depend on how broadly the basic right of equality is defined. It may also depend on its source. Dworkin believes that a rights-based system constructed from the promise of equality promises "the best political program," thus acknowledging the compatibility of his approach with "a fundamental goal that underlies the various popular utilitarian theories."[14] Yet Dworkin rejects one important criterion of classic utilitarianism:

> It is no answer to say that if individuals have these rights [speech, religion, political activity], then the community will be better off in the long run as a whole. This idea—that individual rights may lead to overall utility—may or may not be true, but it is irrelevant to the defence of rights as such, because when we say that someone has a right to speak his mind freely, in the relevant political sense, we mean that he is entitled to do so even if this would not be in the general interest. If we want to defend individual rights in the sense in which we claim them, then we must try to discover something beyond utility that argues for these rights.[15]

But in the absence of any reliance on God, nature, or positive law, is there anything "beyond utility" that is out there waiting to be discovered and that can justify a minority's claimed rights trumping the will of the majority? Though Dworkin believes that a rights-based approach is "best," he would presumably insist on it even if it turned out to be worst! Otherwise, he would be submitting his moral conclusions to the very consequentialist test he eschews. Perhaps Dworkin is saying that although *specific* rights must not be subjected to consequentialist tests, the broad concept of a rights-based system must be justified by the consequentialist test that it is "the best political program." But in the absence of God's voice or nature's mandate, how can we evaluate the claim of rights in general or of any right in particular without weighing it against some utilitarian end—without insisting on some empirical assessment of what is good (or not bad), as judged by agreed-upon criteria? Even the claims of some natural-rights advocates rest—at least to some degree—on the implicit consequentialist assumption that the world will be a better place with eternal natural rights than with only amendable positive rights. A particular right can only be justified as a trump on majority preferences if the recognition of that right will make people better off in the long run[16]—or, conversely, if the non-recognition of that right will make people worse off (which is my preferred negative reformulation of Jeremy Bentham's "greatest happiness of the greatest number" postulate).

If a particular right is part of a package of rights, such as the Bill of Rights, it could be argued that even if that specific right—say the right to bear arms—does not make people better off, they would still be worse off without the package as a whole, and tampering with any particular right may endanger the entire package and make people worse off. (That is why, for example, I would oppose amending the Constitution to eliminate any claimed right to bear arms. My pragmatic fear is that such an amendment would stimulate others to try to "improve" our First Amendment.) But this is simply a variation on rule utilitarianism, as contrasted with act utilitarianism.* It still judges morality by its impact on people—in my formulation, by its impact on preventing the recurrence of wrongs.

Even if Dworkin's logic were impeccable, it would still leave me incompletely satisfied about the source of rights over time and place and the criteria for evaluating their contribution to governance. I find myself accepting his egalitarian postulate (which I see as a recent human *invention* based on the need to prevent the wrongs that flowed from the inequalities of the past), following the logic of where it is supposed to lead me, but then disagreeing—or finding it reasonable for others to disagree—with some of his conclusions. I also wonder whether the postulate is unduly ambiguous, the logic too

---

*See *infra,* at Chapter 10, endnote 3, for definitions of these terms.

one-directional, or the conclusion preordained. Like other brilliant legal philosophers, Dworkin does a better job in criticizing other sources of rights than in coming up with a compelling, stand-alone theory of his own.

In the end Dworkin seems to embrace a variation of natural law, though the embrace is stilted and uncomfortable. By accepting the idea that rights must be "discovered" and by rejecting "utility" as the criterion by which we should judge rights, he seems to be constructing a model of rights based on discoverable "arguments that would justify [certain] claims." This sounds a lot like natural law, despite his refusal to use that loaded term.[17]

In the end, even Dworkin seems to throw up his hands and say, don't worry too much if you can't find a specific source for our rights: We Americans really don't need one because our Constitution is a sufficient source. This subtle shift to positive law does not, as I will show, rescue Dworkin's theory from its limitations.

CHAPTER 5

Do Constitutional Democracies Really Need an External Theory of Rights?

RONALD DWORKIN SUGGESTS that a completely satisfying source for his variation on natural law is not so necessary for a legal philosopher writing about the American system, since in America we have "certain moral rights made into legal rights by the Constitution."[1] Because many of the "natural rights" of our Declaration of Independence have been entrenched by the positive law of our Constitution, there is less of a practical need to deconstruct our rights and obsess about their sources. This approach is consistent with the rhetoric of our Declaration of Independence, which immediately after invoking "unalienable rights" goes on to add that "to secure these rights," we institute government and laws. Most important, we have a written Constitution that has endured, with some important changes, for more than two centuries and is widely regarded as the most successful example of positive law in human history. But if ever our Constitution were to be amended—or our courts to interpret it so as to abrogate these "natural" or Dworkinian rights—we would have to confront the difficult issue of sources and claimed "unalienability." At that point, Dworkin would have the burden of showing why humanly constructed rights, which do not come from God, intuition, or other "ghostly entities," cannot be abrogated by the same humans who constructed (or discovered) them.

Of course, not all our claimed moral rights have been made into legal rights. We must still consider the sources of those claimed rights that do not qualify as both moral and positive. Even the most ardent advocate of natural rights will have to acknowledge that the vast majority of "rights" claimed in any society, including our own, have no basis outside of positive law. There can be no rational claim to a natural right not to have troops quartered in one's home except during wartime. If it became necessary for a government to require every family with extra bedrooms to house a soldier for several months during a period of preparation for a possible war, no one's natural rights would be violated. But absent an abrogation of the Third Amendment, such compelled quartering would violate the positive-law constitutional rights of the homeowner (or renter).

Were the Fifth Amendment's requirement of a grand jury indictment as a prerequisite to federal prosecution to be abrogated in favor of a preliminary hearing requirement, no one's natural rights would be violated (indeed, it would be far better for the rights of most defendants). But at the moment, every federal defendant has a positive-law constitutional right to a grand jury. Even the Supreme Court appears to have recognized the lower status of the grand jury right as compared with, for example, the right to counsel or the privilege against self-incrimination. It "incorporated" the latter rights into the due process clause of the Fourteenth Amendment and applied them to the states as well as to the federal government, but it declined to incorporate the grand jury right, thus leaving the states free to adopt other procedures.

Nor does the warrant requirement of our Fourth Amendment constitute a natural right. Perhaps the general right to privacy, or even the more specific right to be protected against unreasonable searches, may lay claim to being fundamental or even natural. But the warrant requirement grows out of our unique colonial experiences, not from any sense that the warrant procedure provides some talismanic guarantee of reasonableness or privacy. It should not be surprising, therefore, that the warrant requirement is being considerably watered down by the courts, as we grow further removed from the historical experiences that animated it. One might argue that the warrant requirement stands for a broader right to a process that promotes accountability and visibility before government may intrude on privacy, but the specifics of any such right—as enumerated in the Fourth Amendment—are grounded entirely in positive law.

An interesting example of how experience, rather than abstract morality or positive law, determines the content of rights is provided by a case decided by the Supreme Court on June 21, 2004. In that case, the defendant—a farmer with an independent streak—refused to give his name when asked by police who were investigating a report of a domestic assault. The law of Nevada authorized police to demand identification based on "reasonable suspicion" (which is less than "probable cause"). The defendant claimed a constitutional right to privacy under the Fourth Amendment. That amendment is written in somewhat general terms that are subject to varying interpretations. It protects "[t]he right of the people to be secure in their persons . . . against unreasonable searches and seizures. . . ." What constitutes "secure" and "unreasonable" are surely matters of degree that may depend on current threats, historical wrongs, and other experiential factors. These open-textured words invite contemporary courts to strike an appropriate balance between legitimate individual claims of privacy and legitimate governmental claims of effective law enforcement.

Had this case gone to the high court prior to September 11, 2001, the result might well have been different, especially since the trend of previous decisions seemed to favor some right to anonymity in the absence of probable cause.[2] But the proper balance may look different to a judge following the terrible wrongs of 9/11, and especially the perception (if not reality) that these wrongs may have been preventable if proper systems of identification had been in place. The court ruled, in a five-to-four decision, that the "important government interests" in securing the name of suspicious persons outweighed any individual interest in not identifying oneself. Accordingly it refused to recognize a Fourth Amendment right not to disclose one's name when the police reasonably suspect that the person may be involved in criminal conduct.[3]

This is a case that could reasonably have been decided either way under principles of natural law, since it would be difficult to discover in nature an unambiguous right to anonymity. It could also have been decided either way under the principles of interpretation governing positive laws, since the operative words of the Constitution are open to multiple interpretations. The decisive factor in the court's decision to rule for the government was likely our experience with terrorism and the perceived absence of an effective identification system.

Moving on to another provision of our constitutional positive law, some might argue that the right to a jury trial in a serious criminal case is fundamental in the United States, but it is surely not a natural right, given that few other countries accept it. Indeed, it would be difficult to make the case that any particular right of criminal defendants is natural. The most that might be claimed is that basic fairness—by whatever means it is achieved—is a fundamental right that some may wish to characterize as natural. Such basic fairness might include independent decision-makers (whether judge, jury, or some combination), the right to present a defense with the assistance of counsel, placing a burden on the prosecution to prove its case, some avenue for appeal, and protection against excessively cruel punishments (which might vary over time and circumstances). These issues are particularly important today, as efforts are under way to curtail many of these rights, especially in the context of terrorism. The fundamental right denied to the post-9/11 detainees is basic fairness as a check on the arbitrariness of the executive branch.[4]

The right to private ownership of property was certainly deemed fundamental and perhaps even natural by the framers of our Constitution. They entrenched a provision into the Bill of Rights precluding the government from taking property without just compensation. Since that time, however, many good and decent countries—along with some bad and indecent ones—have expropriated some private property for public uses without paying just compensation. Even in our country, cities and states have imposed restrictive zoning laws that have diminished the value of private property, without having to pay compensation. In Massachusetts, private citizens may own their own oceanfront beaches. Many citizens are outraged by the denial of access to what they regard as our collective public seashore. Because of the limited amount of oceanfront in Massachusetts, the value of such beaches has skyrocketed to the point that the state could not now afford to buy them at market value for public use. Were the legislature to enact a law providing a phaseout of private ownership of ocean beaches—say over a twenty-year period or the lifetime of its present owners—there would surely be a constitutional challenge based on the "takings" clause of the Fifth Amendment. But it would be difficult to make the case for a natural right to future private ownership of ocean beaches, or market-value compensation for their taking.

Even the right to transfer wealth from one generation to another—a right once deemed fundamental by my dear friend and late colleague Robert Nozick—is hard to characterize as natural or inalienable. A decent society could, in my view, decide that the fairest way of dealing with wealth is to require each generation to start anew (or relatively anew), be free to accumulate wealth during that generation, and then return all (or some, or most) to the state upon the death of all members of that generation. This may be a foolish, unworkable, or even wrongheaded approach, but if it were to prove, over time, to constitute an improvement—by agreed-upon criteria—over our current approach, it would be difficult to call it unnatural, even if a court were to find it unconstitutional.* Or put more negatively, if some sort of limitation on intergenerational wealth transfer, such as an estate tax, were to help mitigate a significant wrong—such as the perpetuation of a hereditary aristocracy that could eventually undermine democratic rule—a powerful argument could be made against what was once deemed to be a fundamental right.

The Second Amendment provides that "A well-regulated militia, being necessary to the security of a free State, the right of the people to keep and bear Arms, shall not be infringed." The National Rifle Association reads these words as establishing a broad-based natural right to be armed in order to resist governmental tyranny by "throwing off" despotic regimes. Gun-control advocates read the preamble to the amendment—especially the reference to a "well-regulated militia"—as limiting the right to the possession of weapons for military use by the elected government.[5] They also argue that the words "well-regulated" suggest reasonable regulation of gun ownership, such as licensing, waiting periods, and mandatory gun locks. If the militia must be well regulated, it follows—according to this argument—that the private possession of weapons for use in the militia must also be well regulated. The constitutional issue—what the framers "intended" more than two hundred years ago by their somewhat confusing choice of language—will never be resolved to the satisfaction of all sides. But the claim of private, unregulated gun ownership as a natural right is difficult to defend, since it is a uniquely American right,

---

*Nozick modified some of his views relating to property that he first expressed in *Anarchy, State, and Utopia* (Oxford: Clarendon, 1981). Nozick is a wonderful example of a brilliantly intuitive philosopher who combined a priori insights with experiences and history and modified some of his views with changing experiences.

growing out of our colonial experiences. To the extent that it is premised on some right to revolt against democratically elected leaders, it would seem inconsistent with the rule of law, which is also claimed by some as a natural right.

Blackstone includes the right of gun ownership as basic, but many former British colonies, with experiences different from our own, have downgraded this "right." It is not surprising that the written (and unwritten) constitutions of most other nations do not include private gun ownership among the fundamental rights of citizens. Mexico and Switzerland do have a "right to bear arms," and in both countries this right is subject to extensive regulation. According to Japanese law, "no one shall possess a firearm or a sword." In most other countries, gun ownership is severely restricted and few citizens own firearms or believe they have any right to do so. This does not necessarily disqualify a given right from being deemed fundamental or even natural, but it surely supports the view that many rights derive from the unique experiences of a people and can hardly be deemed universal.

If the right to bear arms is narrowed to include only the right to defend oneself and one's family—thus excluding the right to revolt, hunt, collect guns, and possess them for other reasons—a stronger case can be made for its near-universality, despite the fact that some Quakers deny it. But the right to self-defense is generally limited to specific threats and requires that there be no reasonable alternative. It does not extend to the private possession of guns for use in the hypothetical event of lethal aggression, and it certainly does not extend anywhere near where the National Rifle Association would locate it.

For some gun zealots, there is even a right to deny the government information about gun ownership, because despotic governments could use this information to suppress revolution. After the United States had detained nearly 1,000 Arab and Muslim individuals in the wake of September 11, 2001, the F.B.I. requested the gun purchase records of these detainees from the Justice Department.

Attorney General John Ashcroft denied the F.B.I. request, based on his interpretation of the Brady gun-control law. A Justice Department official justified the decision in a written statement: "Being a suspected member of a terrorist organization doesn't disqualify a person from owning a gun any more than being under investigation for a non-terrorism felony would."[6] For the attorney general, who is a strong supporter of the National Rifle Association, the right of an individual to have his gun purchase records remain private seems more important than his right to be free from detention or to challenge his detention in court. As Senator Frank R. Lautenberg put it: "This policy is mind-boggling. We could have a nationwide lookout for a known terrorist within our borders, but if he obtained a weapon, the Justice Department's policy is to refuse to reveal his location to law enforcement officials."

It would seem clear, therefore, that many of the rights contained in our Constitution are simply positive, homegrown rights with roots in the unique American experience, rather than natural rights with legitimate claims to transcending positive law.* The opposite is also true. The "right" of the fetus to live, though deemed natural and universal by many, is not recognized by our Constitution. To the contrary, the Supreme Court, in purporting to construe the Constitution, has given the pregnant woman the "right" to abort—that is, to end the life of—the fetus, at least during certain stages of the pregnancy. According to some natural-law advocates, this ruling (*Roe v. Wade* and its progeny) is not and cannot be the law, since the natural right of the fetus transcends any positive-law enactment. Even were the Constitution to be amended to specify the right of the pregnant woman to abort her fetus, that amendment—though properly enacted—would not be the law, according to this view. There is even a fringe political party in the United States that calls itself the Natural Law Party, which

---

*I will be discussing several other rights in Part II.

seeks to amend the Constitution or overrule its current interpretation so as to bring it into conformity with their view of natural law. A few extremists would go even further and defy the law, or even attack those who exercise their positive rights under it.

Some on the opposite side of the political spectrum make a similar point with regard to the right of a pregnant woman to reproductive freedom, including the choice to abort "her" fetus. They argue that if the Constitution were amended to guarantee the right to life to every fetus (or even only to late-term fetuses), such an amendment would violate the natural right of the woman to control her body. A classic study of abortion concluded that women's attitudes toward the "right to life" versus "the right to choose" are largely a function of their socioeconomic status and life experiences, rather than any abstract commitment to a particular theory of rights.[7] That study "demonstrates that the controversy derives its intensity not from differences of ideology or religion but from the radically antithetical social circumstances of the combatants."[8]

Similar arguments have been made on behalf of the right of homosexuals to have sex with other consenting adults. It is still a crime in some countries for homosexuals to have sex with each other, as it was in several American states before our Supreme Court struck down these laws in 2003 as violations of the right to sexual autonomy and privacy.[9] The Louisiana Supreme Court had upheld its sodomy law as recently as 2000. Many gays, claiming a fundamental right to sexual privacy and autonomy, argued—even before the recent Supreme Court decision—that these anachronistic statutes are not the law, and they disobeyed them with a clear conscience. (Gays generally stay away from invoking "natural law," since that phrase has so often been used against gay rights, especially by religious groups; indeed, sodomy has been called a crime "against nature.")

Thus, despite Dworkin's correct observation that in America we have "certain moral rights made into legal rights by the Constitution," there are many instances of moral rights that did not make the positive-law cut and of other rights that did make it into our Constitution but that can more fairly be characterized as experientially based rights of Americans than as universal or natural rights that transcend positive law. It follows, therefore, that a legal philosopher who seeks to claim for Americans some rights that are not included in the Constitution has some burden of identifying the source of these rights. No one, in my view, has ever convincingly discovered, discerned, constructed, or demonstrated a secular source for his or her theory of natural rights. Nor has Dworkin pinpointed the source of his equality postulate, other than in the brilliant arguments he is capable of making. But arguments alone are not a compelling source, especially for those equally capable of making brilliant counterarguments.

The quest for a compelling secular source of rights is particularly urgent today, because current efforts to alienate so many rights in the name of fighting terrorism (and in the name of God) are being mounted by powerful groups. The arguments of those who would subordinate certain rights to the needs of national security cannot simply be dismissed. Nor can they be answered by invoking God, nature, or logical postulates, since such ethereal concepts are unpersuasive to so many reasonable people. As my late friend and colleague John Hart Ely once put it, "The advantage [of natural law and its variations] is that you can invoke [it] to support anything you want. The disadvantage is that everyone understands that."[10] To which I would add that the advantage is often regained by natural-law advocates because so many who favor the outcome they claim is mandated by natural law pretend not to understand its intellectual bankruptcy. As the scholar Benjamin Wright has wisely observed, "in the heat of controversies," it is "the winning of a cause, not the discussion of problems of ontology, which occupies men's minds."[11]

Do We Need to Invent an External Source of Rights—Even If It Does Not Really Exist?

ONE OF THE most compelling—and frequently heard—arguments for invoking natural law is that we *need* it! Without it, we have no basis—at least no legal basis—for opposing or resisting unjust laws that have been properly enacted.

I have often heard very smart people pose the following rhetorical question: "O.K., you may have persuaded me rationally that there are no external sources of rights—that God, nature, postulates of equality, strongboxes, collective wills are all too vague and ethereal. But where does that leave us?"

They point out that human beings have proved themselves incapable of governing without some perceived outside source of morality and rights. Absent such a source, there are no limits to what we are willing to do to each other. We need constraints, and we need to believe that these restraints come from some higher authority and are objectively binding on us. If that external source does not really exist or does not speak in moral terms, we must still act as if it did. We need the moral fiction of a higher authority, even if we have to make it up. We crave "miracle, mystery, and authority," as Dostoyevsky put it in his masterful Grand Inquisitor scene:

Nothing has ever been more insupportable for a man and a human society than freedom. If they begin to build their tower of Babel without us [the church authority] they will end, of course, with cannibalism.

Even H. L. A. Hart, a persistent critic of natural law and proponent of a modified version of morally infused positive law, acknowledges the need for some external guarantee of fundamental rights. Citing the horrors of the mid-twentieth century, he observes that "a theory of rights is urgently called for," lest we repeat our tragic history.[1] This is, of course, an empirical claim that is purportedly based on the collective experiences of humankind: Without external sources of morality, catastrophe potentially ensues. And it may well be accurate. It also purportedly derives from the nature of human beings: We need external sources of morality because without them we cannot resist the temptations of freedom.

Rabbi Joseph Telushkin put it even more pointedly: "To this day there is ultimately no philosophically compelling answer to the question 'Why was Hitler wrong?' aside from 'Because God said so.'"*

The argument for an external source of rights thus seems to boil down to the old saw: "You can't live with it, and you can't live without it." You can't live with it because it simply doesn't exist. You can't live without it because the consequences of its nonexistence are frightening.

The "need" argument for natural law is strikingly similar to the functional argument for God and religion. We *need* God to set limits on our actions. Again the Grand Inquisitor: "If there is no God,

---

*Joseph Telushkin, *Jewish Wisdom* (New York: Morrow, 1994), p. 43. I try to show in this book that Rabbi Telushkin is wrong—that an atheist or an agnostic also has a basis for condemning Hitler based on experience. It was experience with the wrongs of genocide, not theological arguments, that led to the post–World War II burgeoning of human rights.

all is permitted." We *need* God in order to make sense of our existence and to assign us a purpose. We *need* external authority to free us of the internal anxiety of untrammeled choice.[2] We *need* religion in order to deal with life's tragedies and its inevitable end. We *need* an afterlife to rationalize the injustices of this life and to serve as an incentive to good behavior and a disincentive to bad.[3] Voltaire, who himself did not believe in God, wanted his lawyer, his valet, and his wife to believe in God, because if they do, "I shall be . . . cheated less."

There are no atheists in a foxhole—or on a crashing airplane, we are assured. Maybe not. But the need argument no more proves the actual existence of God than it proves the existence of an external source of natural law or natural rights. Just because we need something does not prove that this something actually exists. What it may prove is that we need to pretend it exists or to create it, construct it, or invent it. Hart, who acknowledges the need, has correctly observed that enormous energy has recently been devoted to the quest for a "sufficiently firm foundation" for a theory of basic, inalienable rights.[4] But "need" plus energetic quest do not always produce satisfaction. We need to cure cancer and we are devoting enormous resources to our quest for the cure, but we have not yet satisfied this need, and there is no assurance we will.

Likewise with the quest to satisfy the need for an external source of basic rights: The difference is that we will never find the latter, because it does not exist. Just as human beings created an intervening God, organized religion, and the afterlife, so, too, have we created divine natural law, secular natural law, and other moral and legal fictions deemed essential to satisfy some of our most basic and enduring needs. As Dostoyevsky's Grand Inquisitor put it: "The universal and everlasting craving of humanity [is] to find someone to worship. So long as man remains free, he strives for nothing so incessantly and so painfully as to find someone to worship." This is the "fundamental secret of human nature"—that "man is tormented by no greater anxiety than to find someone quickly to whom he can hand over that great gift of freedom with which the ill-fated creature is born."[5]

To the extent that this creative process is thought to grow out of some set of inherent human needs, it may be called natural. To the extent that it grows out of the experiences of human beings over time, it may be called experiential or nurtural. The line between the two may not be sharp, since experiences often reflect inherent or deeply rooted aspects of human nature. Human experience may well prove the need for an external source of rights, but it does not establish that such a source actually exists.

A prominent example of the need for natural law was the American quest for independence. British control of the colonies was legitimated by repeated acts of Parliament. It was lawful, at least according to English positive law. But Jefferson asserted that there was a higher law—the law of Nature and of Nature's God—that trumped English positive law, especially since the colonists were not represented in the English Parliament (as many, probably most, other British subjects were not represented in those days of limited suffrage). Those who opposed the Slave Codes, the Nuremburg laws, and the Stalinist Constitution (as interpreted by the KGB courts) also invoked a higher law because they had no alternative, in the absence of any positive law that supported their claim to fundamental fairness and decency. They truly *needed* natural law.

It is one thing to say that natural law is a useful, even essential, legal fiction for a civilized world (more of that in the next chapter). It is quite another thing to say it actually exists. Until and unless a cure for breast cancer actually comes into existence, it is fraudulent and dangerous to pretend that we have one. The truth is that a set of specific rights based on natural law simply does not exist, no matter how much we "need" it or wish it did. Natural law is a human invention, much like religions that believe in an intervening God. And it may be beneficial or harmful, much like such religions. (I will address that question in the next chapter as well.) But even if it is beneficial, that doesn't make it any more real than a placebo.

There are, after all, only three basic sources of human knowledge: discovery, invention, and revelation.[6] The physical rules of nature actually exist, and await discovery by human beings. (They would, of course, exist even in the absence of human beings, as they did for billions of years. They just would not be called "rules," because there would be no one to understand or even name them.) Newton discovered some, Einstein others, and Darwin yet others. If these giants had not discovered these rules when they did, it is reasonable to assume that other geniuses would have made these (or similar) discoveries, since the rules of nature are out there waiting to be discovered, just as some European would have found the Mississippi River even if Hernando de Soto had somehow missed it.[7] Jerry Seinfeld, it turns out, was right.

Inventions are different.* They require the creative combining of different kinds of knowledge and information—both theoretical and practical—to design something that did not previously exist. Simple inventions, such as the cotton gin or the internal combustion engine, would have been made by others, if those responsible for inventing them had never lived. Complex, more individualistic inventions, such as Beethoven's symphonies, Picasso's paintings, and Shakespeare's plays, would never have been replicated by others, at least not exactly. They are truly unique.** We call them "inspired," but they are human inventions. There are also, of course, many things that fall somewhere between discovery and invention, and

---

*Inventions are generally dependent on discoveries, and the lines between them are often blurred.

**It is likely that even in the absence of Picasso, someone would have invented an approach to modern art similar to his. The same can be said for Beethoven and classical music and Shakespeare and the inner life of dramatic characters, but it wouldn't be quite the same.

there are overlaps. This is because inventions often require discoveries, and vice versa.

Finally there is divine revelation, for those who believe in it. (It is claimed to be a genre of discovery, but to skeptics it is pure human invention.) Like discovery and invention, revelation lies along a continuum. Some people believe that God actually spoke to particular human beings, handed them tablets, or dictated entire books. Others believe that God inspires human conduct, in ways that are not subject to human understanding. Yet others, like Jefferson and his fellow Deists, believed that God created the rules of both physical and human nature, and that any human being, by observing these rules, can see God's will revealed (discovered) without the intermediation of churches, bibles, or ministers.

What then are laws, rights, and morality? Positive law is plainly a human invention. Madison's Constitution, for example, with its emphasis on checks and balances, is an experiment based on human experience—mostly negative—with other types of government. As Churchill later said of democracy: "Indeed, it has been said that democracy is the worst form of Government except all those other forms that have been tried from time to time." This too was based on human experience, especially on the wrongs produced by other forms of government. Our Constitution—with its system of checks and balances—was an attempt to improve on the past. Like most human inventions, it was built on prior inventions and discoveries. Also like most inventions, it is imperfect and requires a process for its own change and improvement.

Natural law, on the other hand, purports to be a product of discovery and/or revelation. It is out there somewhere, fully developed and flawless, simply waiting to be discovered or discerned by human beings so that they can live by its principles. Jefferson and many of his contemporaries believed that human beings, by employing their God-given senses, could discover external truths. But as Jeremy Bentham once observed in a related context: This is "nonsense on stilts." There is simply nothing out there waiting to be discovered, certainly nothing perfect and unchanging. All laws, in the sense of prescriptive rules of conduct and morality, are imperfect and ever-changing human inventions, for which we, as their inventors, are ultimately responsible. Natural law, and all of its variations, are also human inventions, dressed up by humans as discoveries and revelations to give them greater authority. They are, ultimately, no more than legal or moral fictions.

At the very least, this is what many people throughout the world honestly believe. They also believe that rights are essential to democratic governance. For these people (and I count myself among them) it is important to know where these rights come from—what are their sources—especially since they trump majority rule. It is not enough to pretend that they derive from some external source that does not exist or cannot be understood. If rights are to trump majority rule, they must have a status higher than simple democracy, as well as a source beyond positive law. Moreover, human experience has demonstrated that the moral fictions of divine and natural law often do more harm than good. If that is true, then we should get on with the business of devising a theory of rights based on humanly accessible sources and subject to truth-testing mechanisms accessible to all.

CHAPTER 7

Is Natural Law a Helpful or Harmful Fiction?

IN ADDITION TO the question of whether natural law is a fiction—a human invention—there is the question of whether natural law is a beneficial or harmful fiction. Because it is a fiction—a human invention—it has a heavy burden to establish its usefulness. If it cannot satisfy the burden of proving that it does more good than harm, it should be discarded.* When natural law is invoked to produce a "good" result—to persuade individuals not to obey the "lawful" commands of evil tyrants—we all approve it (ironically because we conclude that the end justifies the means—a very nonnatural-law criterion for evaluating anything!). But we must remind ourselves that natural law has also been invoked in support of slavery, racism, sexism, homophobia, terrorism, the blocking of abortion clinics, and the refusal to pay taxes.

At bottom, natural law is an invitation to self-righteous lawlessness (both positive and negative), in the sense that it provides a justification for refusing to obey the positive law. We applaud such lawlessness when it is directed against evil, but condemn it when it leads to evil. The inherent problem is that natural law is a double-edged sword

---

*Even if a fiction can satisfy a utilitarian burden, honesty may compel us to discard it. But if it cannot meet this utilitarian onus, there is hardly an argument for its preservation.

aimed at the heart of democracy and the rule of law, since these important mechanisms necessarily rely on positive law that is equally accessible to all. Natural law, on the other hand, relies on elitist messages from God and nature that are not accessible to anyone but those who claim an ability to hear the voice of the divinity or interpret the moral lessons of nature. They are anything but self-evident.

Jefferson needed a source outside of the law as a trump, and at the time he was writing the Declaration of Independence, natural law was seen as that trump by people who rejected biblical law, as Jefferson did. Indeed, in those days, natural law was seen by secular radicals such as Rousseau, Spinoza, and Leibniz as the progressive alternative to divinely revealed biblical law. It was progressive in several senses: First, it was available to all who could observe nature—it was "self-evident"—and did not require bibles, churches, prophets, priests, or government officials to translate or interpret the revealed word of God; second, its content was not fixed by the dead hand of the past, which all too often justified tyranny, authority, and repression; and third, these progressive proponents of natural law could infuse it with "good" natural rights, as Jefferson did with the right to secede and the rights of life, liberty, and the pursuit of happiness.

An example of Jefferson's elitist use of natural law and natural rights to thwart majority preferences is provided by his noble effort at preventing future amendments to one of his most important contributions to positive law. In his 1779 "Bill for Establishing Religious Freedom," Jefferson included a section containing the following admonition to future legislators:

> . . . though we well know that this Assembly elected by the people for the ordinary purposes of legislation only, have no power to restrain the acts of succeeding Assemblies, constituted with powers equal to our own, and that therefore to declare this act irrevocable would be

> of no effect in law; yet we are free to declare, and do declare, that the
> rights hereby asserted are of the natural rights of mankind, and that
> if any act shall be hereafter passed to repeal the present or to narrow
> its operation, such act will be an infringement of natural right.

Thus, instead of trying to persuade the governed to make it difficult, by positive law, to amend the right to religious liberty, Jefferson invoked a higher law: "natural rights."

In support of his claimed natural right to religious freedom, Jefferson argued that if God, who is all-powerful, wanted everyone to follow the same religion, they would. He believed it was a natural right of humankind not to be compelled "to furnish contributions of money for the propagation of opinions which he disbelieves" and to "be free to profess, and by argument to maintain, their opinion in matters of religion."[1] I certainly agree that such rights *should* be recognized, indeed entrenched, by the law, since experience demonstrates that if they are not recognized many evils will follow. But these rights do not come from nature. Even if the opposite were "natural"—even if there were a genetic or intuitive predisposition toward believing in and imposing one true religion—I would still argue for the right to religious freedom and dissent, based on experience with the wrongs of religious tyranny and censorship. Most people die with the same religion into which they were born, and many believe that their religion is the true one. Catholicism, Puritanism, and Islam, among others, have long advocated mandatory contributions to propagate their faith and punishment for those who advocate a different one. Jefferson's rights are important, not because human nature supports them, but because it does *not*. The right to dissent from the consensus of religious or other views reflects anti-natural law—*nurtural* law—at its best. It is the function of rights to change human nature, or at least to provide a counterpoint to nature, based on human experience.

Jefferson sought to codify into positive law what he had discovered in natural law. He was not alone in his effort to combine the two traditional sources of rights. Madison did the same with the Constitution. In fact, almost no one trusts natural or divine law itself to influence conduct without the threat of positive-law sanctions. Even churches codify their rules and punish their violation. This raises the following question: If neither natural law standing alone nor positive law standing alone provides a compelling source of rights, do these two working in tandem serve as an adequate basis for rights? The answer must clearly be no, because the tandem approach provides no criteria for resolving conflicts between natural and positive law. Advocates of natural law insist that because of the superior status of its source—God, nature, or some other higher authority—natural law must always trump positive law. Advocates of positive law maintain that its source—democracy and the rule of law—gives it a higher status. Hence we are inevitably brought back to the truth of, the need for, or at least the benefit brought by, natural law—if it is to trump positive law.

For every historical example of a benevolent use of natural law, such as those represented by Jefferson, one can cite multiple malignant uses. Patrick Buchanan, for example, has characterized AIDS as "nature's revenge" against gay men for their "unnatural" and "immoral" behavior. An ultra-orthodox rabbi in Israel declared the Holocaust to be God's punishment of the Jews for eating pork. Former presidential candidate Alan Keyes has told high school students that belief in evolution entails the conclusion that "might makes right," and leads women to abort their children.

In a July 2004 debate on the U.S. Senate floor over gay marriage, the following natural-law argument was often heard:

The function of marriage is procreative;
The laws of nature require a man and woman to create life;

It follows therefore that marriage must be between a man and a woman.

There are so many flaws in this argument—logical, empirical, experiential, moral, even religious—that it is difficult to know where to begin. In the first place the premise is simply false, as proved by the fact that no one—not even the most fundamentalist religious leader—would outlaw the marriage of an infertile couple. Adoption is a common response to infertility, and eighty-year-olds marry every day, with the blessings of their churches. Some say miracles are possible. If they are—if the ninety-year-old Sarah could give birth to Isaac or the virgin Mary could conceive Jesus—then why can't two lesbian women have a child as well? And what will happen when cloning permits reproduction by a single person? Will that change in the law of nature require a change in the eternal moral laws of marriage?

The same laws of nature that currently require a man and a woman (or at least a sperm and an egg) for conception also explain the sexual attraction of some men for other men and some women for other women—as well as the need for companionship.

Moreover, no one would argue that just because thirteen-year-olds can make babies, they should be permitted to marry, or that rapists who impregnate their victims should be required to marry them (as the Bible mandates). There is no necessary correlation between the natural ability to procreate and the right to marry. Many of the same people and institutions that oppose gay marriage today also opposed miscegenation, despite the reality that mixed-race couples can surely procreate. They cited nature's abhorrence of "mongrel" children and the dire threat to "white" society. Nature often provides a cover for bigotry.

The "is" of nature should not dictate the "ought" of law or morality, though it must surely be taken into account. Moreover, the progress (and sometimes regress) of science and technology is amending the laws of nature at a rapid pace. What was naturally impossible in generations past has become scientifically feasible today, and who knows what the future holds.

The argument from nature cannot, of course, be used against adoption by gay and lesbian couples—at least not the same reductionist biological argument that is offered against gay marriage. Not only *can* such couples adopt, but experience has shown that they can make wonderful parents—not in every case, but that is also true of heterosexual couples. Yet many Americans, including President George W. Bush, would deny gay and lesbian couples the right to adopt, citing natural law. Here there is a direct clash between human experience and natural law (as defined by some) that can actually be resolved by research. It is certainly possible to conduct a double-blind experiment, with agreed-upon criteria, to determine whether gay and lesbian parents are considerably "worse" than heterosexual parents, as opponents of gay and lesbian adoption claim. I doubt that these opponents would be satisfied by the results of such an experiment, since they too may be using nature as a cover for bigotry.

The views expressed by the traditionalists cited above are, of course, something of a caricature of serious thinking with regard to natural law and natural rights. But I have neither read nor heard any persuasive account of natural law or rights that, in the end, is not a dressed-up version of "my politics (religion, ideology, economic self-interest, etc.) is right and yours is wrong because God (who you can't hear) says so, or nature (which does not speak in the language of morality) points us there."

Experience demonstrates that natural law, like other legal fictions, can be, and has been, used to justify many evils. In theory it can also be used to counteract evils, but the experiences of the twentieth century raise serious concerns about the actual utility of natural law, especially during times of crisis. That century's history includes some of the worst abuses of human rights ever committed by governments, including the Holocaust, the deliberate starvation of Ukrainians, the massacres by and of Cambodians, the genocide against Armenians, and others. These cataclysmic events challenged conventional theories of religion, law, and morality, especially those based on divine or natural law, but also those based on positive law. How could an intervening, omniscient, omnipotent, and good God have permitted the Holocaust?[2] Is it in the nature of human beings to stand silently by as millions of innocent civilians, including children, are murdered? Why did the Catholic Church, which claims the mantle of natural law, do so little to prevent genocide? How could so many great thinkers—from Heidegger to Heisenberg—have accepted the morality of Nazism?

For a lawyer who rejects natural law, the challenge is particularly acute. What is the alternative? The Germans were scrupulous about enacting their laws with great attention to procedural niceties and formalities.[3] For legal positivists, this raises challenging questions: Were the Nuremberg racial laws—which denied Jews and others basic rights—"the law"? Did Jews actually lose all of their rights? Or did there continue to exist, outside of enacted German law, a set of legal and moral rights that the victims of the Nuremberg laws could claim and seek to enforce? The inconclusive answers to these questions are complex and give no more solace to supporters of natural law than to advocates of positive law. The reality is that the victims of Nazism had no legal rights in fact—and certainly no legal remedies—while in Germany and Nazi-occupied Europe.* They and their supporters urged those who could still exercise some power or influence over Germany—religious, moral, economic, military, diplomatic, or other—to do so in a moral way so as to try to save

---

*I do not regard the *forms* of legality as bestowing actual rights, when the outcome was predetermined by the ideology.

them. But these appeals generally failed, because self-serving practical considerations were deemed more pressing.[4]

In the end, natural law did little to prevent the abuses of Nazi positive law when it might have mattered—during the war itself. Though the Catholic Church has traditionally been the most articulate exponent of a transcendent, divinely based natural law, the Vatican, as an institution, did little to articulate a natural-law imperative to oppose Nazi law. The pope failed as a moral leader. When he was asked by the Berlin correspondent of the Vatican newspaper, *L'Osservatore Romano*, if he would not protest against the extermination of the Jews, Pius reportedly replied, "Dear friend, do not forget that millions of Catholics serve in the German armies. Shall I bring them into conflicts of conscience?"[5]

If it is not the job of the chief spokesman for natural law and morality to create "conflicts of conscience" in those who are violating such law and morality in the most fundamental way, what is his role? (By the way, the Vatican has never had a problem bringing Catholic lawmakers who represent constituents that support a woman's right to choose abortion or a gay couple's right to live together into "conflicts of conscience.") And if it is not the role of natural law to serve as a check on barbarities like those of the laws of Nazism, what function is natural law supposed to serve? Nor was the failure of the Catholic Church limited to passive silence. It was actively complicit in some of the most egregious violations of natural law, including the employment of slave laborers allocated to German Catholic institutions by Nazis.[6] Natural law, especially divine natural law, cannot excuse its failures by claiming that it cannot be expected to work during periods of crisis or emergency. These are precisely the situations in which natural law makes its greatest claims to superiority over human law.

In the pope's defense, some have pointed to pragmatic concerns, such as preventing the victory of communism, preserving church property, and even saving the lives of priests. But it is the claimed virtue of natural law and morality that it does not employ cost-benefit analysis or situational ethics. Yet that is precisely what is claimed on behalf of Pope Pius XII, who is on the road to canonization. Elevating Pius XII to sainthood would announce to future generations that tactical silence in the face of immorality will be rewarded—even decades after the crisis has passed—by those who claim to champion natural law. Others argue that the failure of *this* particular embodiment of natural law to live up to its demanding and uncompromising standards does not mean that natural law, as an ideal concept, is bankrupt. But those who advocate natural law as a check on positivism at least have the burden of demonstrating that it has worked during times that test the souls of men and women. The experiences of humankind do not appear to satisfy that burden.

Events such as the Holocaust raise questions not so much about the *sources* of the law as about its *scope,* power, and reach. I believe the Nuremberg racial laws, which were "properly" enacted within Germany, violated positive international law and the norms of human morality. All civilized nations condemned what the Nazis were doing in the name of German law (though few acted on that condemnation). They could not enforce their more elevated notions of international law and morality until after the war was over and the Nazi leaders were tried at Nuremberg.

But what if all the nations of the world agreed that it is permissible to kill the Jews, to enslave blacks, or to eat children? Would that make it "law" and deny these victims any claim of right? To what source of authority could the victims then point? The postwar Nuremberg tribunal sought to answer these questions by recognizing and imposing a set of fundamental rules designed by human beings to transcend the positive laws of individual nations.[7] This effort has not been without its difficulties, conceptually and practically, especially when the "new" positive law has been applied retroactively

to acts that occurred before its articulation. But it has made a difference. There have been some trials and convictions of those who
acted in violation of international positive law, though their actions
were in accord with their own domestic positive law.[8] Nuremberg
thus stands for both ends of the legal and moral continuum. The
very laws enacted at Nuremberg during the Nazi regime were placed
on trial at Nuremberg immediately after the war. The original
Nuremberg laws proved to be no defense to the higher positive law
imposed by the victorious nations, and this now serves as a positive-
law precedent throughout the world. Although the precedent is
often difficult to enforce, the world of international human rights is
in a different place today than it was a century ago.

For those who share Jeremy Bentham's skeptical view—"nonsense on stilts," he called all moral rights—my answer is that he may
have been correct as a matter of descriptive fact, especially at the
time he was writing in the eighteenth and early nineteenth centuries. This means that we must try harder. It is our responsibility as
advocates of international human rights to persuade the world
community that it is better to live in a world governed by rights than
one ruled by force, just as it is better to live in a nation governed by
rights rather than in one ruled by power alone. This is our challenge, especially in an age of globalized communication, where no
one can any longer plausibly present the excuse claimed by most decent people during the Holocaust: "We did not know." Many did
know, or should have known, or could have found out but did not
want to know. As Supreme Court Justice Felix Frankfurter told the
great Jan Karski after listening to Karski's detailed account of the
Warsaw ghetto and the death camps, "A man like me talking to a
man like you must be totally honest. So I am. So I say: I cannot believe you."

He did not say that he *did not* believe it was true but rather that
he *could not* believe it. He and others like him *chose* not to know,

in the interests of self-serving pragmatism. That was nature at work. Our efforts to avoid the recurrence of the Holocaust is nurture at work.

Denial—the refusal to believe—is no longer possible in an age of instant communication, so we must confront directly the difficult issue of how to advocate, implement, and enforce the kinds of basic human rights—most especially the right not to be killed on account of one's race, religion, or ethnicity—that elevate us above species that act only on the "natural" instincts of self-preservation and genetic propagation. In this era of state-sponsored terrorism based on race, ethnicity, and religion, this imperative has taken on a new urgency. The recent terrorism is the kind of "experience" that changes philosophies.

Consider President George W. Bush's justifiable decision to authorize the shooting down of hijacked passenger jets about to crash into occupied buildings. Philosophers have to fit this decision into existing *theories,* because almost everybody now believes it is the proper choice of evils under the circumstances. John Rawls would have little difficulty, since anyone behind a veil of ignorance would favor saving thousands of full lives over hundreds of additional seconds of life. Nor would Bentham hesitate under his utilitarian calculus. But Immanuel Kant would have difficulty, since it would be using one group to save another. A clever Kantian might argue that the passengers would will their own deaths rather than become the instruments of death of so many. But that would not solve the problem for theologians for whom willed death is suicide. If a terminally ill person in pain cannot will his own death before God decides to end his life, how can a passenger hasten his demise to save others?

Theologians will find justifications. They might see an analogy to soldiers who know they will die performing their duty. But what if some of the passengers prefer to try to regain control of the plane? Perhaps there is an analogy to a person being used as a human shield by a criminal firing his gun. The certainty is that the Bush order will be found religiously, philosophically, and legally correct, since no one who wants to be taken seriously will say that the plane should not be shot down. The *constant* is the answer; the *variable* is the reasoning. Our experience with evil (terrorists using jets as bombs) has given us the right answer to what once was a debatable tragic choice. Now we must figure out how to frame the question so as to ensure arriving at this answer. I will argue in the next chapter that the question must be framed not by asking what God or nature teaches us, but rather what experience teaches us.

Much of jurisprudence has been devoted to trying to resolve the intractable conflict between those who advocate natural law (and its variants) and those who espouse legal positivism (and its variants). At the extremes, it is a false dichotomy that pits one illogical approach that seeks to derive moral content from the morally neutral operation of nature against another equally illogical approach that seeks to ascribe morality to humanly enacted laws that may, or may not, be moral.

There are no divine laws of morality, merely human laws claiming the authority of God. Nor are there any moral laws that derive from the nature of man, merely human efforts to control the evils and to promote the goodness of human nature. Any attempt to build a jurisprudence on the word of God or the workings of nature must fail, because neither God nor nature speaks with one voice capable of being heard or understood by humans. Nor can a jurisprudence be built on legal positivism, since that approach to law is bereft of substantive moral content. It is merely descriptive of what the law is, rather than prescriptive of what it ought to be. Finally, no combination of the two will solve the problem, since in the end one must trump the other when there are inevitable conflicts.

In an age when we better understand the randomness of nature—that it has no externally mandated "purpose"—we cannot continue to abdicate our human responsibility to construct a morality that elevates us above our base natural instincts and reinforces our beneficent ones.[9] My late friend and colleague Stephen Jay Gould has put it this way:

> *Homo sapiens* may be the brainiest species of all, but we represent only a tiny twig, grown but yesterday on a single branch of the richly arborescent bush of life. This bush features no preferred direction of growth, while our own relatively small limb of vertebrates ranks only one among many, not even *primus inter pares.* There is nothing special about us. The world is not there for us. We are not the object of creation, but rather the product of random forces.[10]

If he is correct, then the randomness of the universe poses the greatest challenge to human morality. If we are here alone, with no preordained destiny, then it is we—as individuals and as community—who must determine our destiny. We are responsible for our future, as we have been for our past. It is we who must improve upon nature and repair the world. As an ancient Buddhist proverb says: "To every man is given the key to the gates of heaven; the same key opens the gates of hell." It is we who must decide how to use that key.[11] It is we who create morality, for better or worse, because there is no morality "out there" waiting to be discovered or handed down from some mountaintop. It is because I am a skeptic that I am a moralist. It is because there is no morality beyond human invention that we must devote so much energy to the task of building morality, law, and rights. We cannot endure without morality, law, and rights, yet they do not exist unless *we* bring them into existence. We must not abdicate our own decision-making to other human beings who alone claim to hear the silent voice of God or to understand the unknowable moral implications of nature. A great Hasidic rabbi was once asked whether it is ever proper to act as if there were no God.

He replied, "Yes. When a poor man asks you for charity, act as if there is no God—act as if only you can save him from starving." I would extend the rabbi's answer to all moral decisions about repairing the world.*

The time has come to recognize the intellectual bankruptcy of both traditional natural law and traditional legal positivism and to seek a different approach to the relationship between the *is* of nature and the *ought* of morality, as well as between the *is* of existing law and the *ought* of what law should be. As I will show in the next chapter, this approach must rest on the experiences of human beings.

---

*Further, in an age when we have seen the worst abuses of morality done in the name of positive law, we cannot accept the existence of law as an argument for its morality. One can, of course, agree with Socrates that a citizen has a moral obligation to obey laws that were properly enacted by a fair society, though few would contend that Nazi Germany was a fair society.

CHAPTER 8

What, Then, Is the Source of Rights?

IN THE ABSENCE of any external basis, what then remains as a compelling source of rights, other than positive law itself? In sum, the theory presented in this book is that rights are those fundamental preferences that experience and history—especially of great injustices—have taught are so essential that the citizenry should be persuaded to entrench them and not make them subject to easy change by shifting majorities.

In one important respect, therefore, this theory of rights is a theory of wrongs. It begins with the worst injustices: the Crusades, the Inquisition, slavery, the Stalinist starvation and purges, the Holocaust, the Cambodian slaughter, and other abuses that reasonable people now recognize to have been wrongs.

The ongoing nature of the righting process—and the fact that there is no consensus with regard to perfect justice—does not require that we ignore the wrongs of obvious injustice or allow those who advocate or inflict them to fall back on moral relativism as a justification for immorality. There is no moral justification for genocide, as evidenced by the fact that no reasoned argument has ever been attempted on its behalf—certainly none that has succeeded in the marketplace of ideas over time. Even Hitler and his henchmen tried to hide their genocidal actions behind euphemisms and evasive rhetoric.[1] Today we have Holocaust deniers but few if any Holocaust justifiers. Indeed, the Holocaust serves as a paradigm of injustice.

Slavery, too, is such a paradigm. Yet it had its defenders. The arguments made by these defenders have been soundly rejected by the verdict of history, and not only because the slaveholders lost on the battlefield. Even had the South been victorious, the institution of slavery would not have long survived. Economic and moral considerations would have doomed it in the South, as it has been doomed nearly everywhere else in the world. Viewed through the lens of experience, slavery has proved to be a paradigm of injustice despite the contemporaneous arguments of its practitioners and defenders. There is no consensus about what perfect justice would be for those who work for others: A fair wage? A share of the profits? Various types of insurance? Reasonable people can and do disagree about perfect economic justice for employees. But every reasonable person now recognizes that slavery was a grave injustice.

My approach to rights first identifies the most grievous wrongs whose recurrence we seek to prevent, and then asks whether the absence of certain rights contributed to these wrongs. If so, that experience provides a powerful argument for why such rights should become entrenched. This bottom-up approach builds on the reality that there is far more consensus about what constitutes gross injustice than about what constitutes perfect justice. If there can be agreement that certain rights are essential to reduce injustice, such agreement constitutes the beginning of a solid theory of rights. We can continue to debate about the definition of, and conditions for, perfect justice. That debate will never end because perfect justice is far too theoretical and utopian a concept. But in the meantime, we can learn a considerable amount about rights from the world's entirely untheoretical experiences of injustice. Building on this negative experience, we can advocate and implement basic rights that have been shown (or can be shown) to serve as a check on tyranny and injustice. Perhaps someday we will be able to construct a complete theory of rights designed to lead to perfect justice. But since we have had far more experience with palpable injustice than with abstractly perfect justice, the bottom-up approach seems more grounded in reality than any top-down approach. It is more modest in its scope, but if it can contribute to a slowing down of the kind of injustice we have experienced in the twentieth and other centuries, it will have accomplished a great deal.

Aristotle had it upside-down when he argued that before we can define people's rights or investigate "the nature of the ideal constitution . . . it is necessary for us first to determine the nature of the most desirable way of life. As long as that remains obscure, the nature of the ideal constitution must also remain obscure."[2] In my view, it is sufficient to agree upon the *least* desirable ways of life and seek to protect against those evils. Such a minimalist conception of rights may not be "ideal," but it may be the best we can ever hope for. In the millennia since Aristotle wrote, we have come no closer to determining "the nature of the most desirable way of life." Reasonable people will always disagree about the nature of the perfect good, but there will be less disagreement about the evils that experience has taught us to try to prevent.

Rejection of the Aristotelian view requires that the following questions be addressed: In the absence of a theory of justice, how can we recognize its opposite, injustice?* By what standard are we to judge injustice in a world without a paradigm of justice? These are theoretical questions that may have no perfect theoretical answer.

---

*In my last conversation with my dear friend and teaching colleague Robert Nozick, Bob raised the question of how I could know what perfect injustice was without first defining perfect justice. Although there is no completely satisfying answer to this probing question, I do think it is possible to recognize significant injustices without having a conception of perfect justice.

But the fact remains that experience has taught us to recognize, if not *perfect* injustice, then certainly gross types of injustice that no one—at least no one today—would try to justify. What constitutes perfect justice remains debatable among decent and intelligent people today, but no such people would debate the injustice of the Holocaust or other instances of deliberate, mass genocide. We have seen injustice and we now know it, even if some did not know it at the time it was being perpetrated.* Perhaps if we were ever to experience perfect justice, we would know that too, but as of now we have never come close to that experience. The utopian philosophers failed to achieve consensus over what a perfectly just society would be like, even in theory. It has been easier for writers of dystopias to describe injustice—as in Orwell's *1984,* Huxley's *Brave New World,* and Kafka's *The Trial*—than to imagine perfect justice. This more modest approach to rights may not only be the best we can do, but in a diverse society with differing conceptions of the best life, it may be the "ideal constitution."

In any event, the very notion of "perfect" justice is an abstraction that itself derives from "perfect" external sources, like God and nature. René Descartes argued that only God is perfect[3] and that the imperfect can be understood only as a referent to the perfect.[4] But in seeking to prevent recurrence of grievous wrongs, we need not limit ourselves to combating perfect injustice. It is enough to recognize serious injustices that are down-to-earth, real, and generally produced by imperfect human beings. Moreover, the need to reduce

---

*The late Justice Potter Stewart once quipped that although he could not define hardcore pornography, "I know it when I see it." It is remarkable to me that some people today do not acknowledge the injustice of terrorism, arguing that some forms of terrorism are justifiable or that some noble ends justify the use of terrorism as a means. Even these people seem to agree that at least certain acts of terrorism—such as those directed against the World Trade Center—constitute injustice.

it is practical and immediate. We need not agree on what constitutes "perfect injustice" in order to build a pragmatic theory of rights (which does not itself claim perfection). It is enough to agree on what constitutes the kinds of injustices that are sufficiently wrong to occasion a system of rights designed to prevent their recurrence. Seeking to achieve the perfect is the enemy of trying to prevent the very bad.

Building a theory of rights on the history of wrongs has another important virtue. It is a call to immediate action. We need not await the arrival of the Aristotelian Messiah—agreement on "the most desirable way of life"—before we can begin to confront the wrongs we all seek to prevent. While we wait for this Messiah (along with others), many horrible wrongs will be committed, some in his name. As soon as we see such wrongs, and decide to prevent their recurrence, our mission becomes clear: Invent and advocate rights designed to stop (or slow down) these wrongs. The Aristotelian approach is an invitation to inaction. An approach that bases rights on wrongs is a demand for immediate action.

It is also a demand for continuing advocacy of rights. If rights do not come from static sources, such as an eternal God or His unchangeable laws of nature, then we must constantly defend our choice of rights by reference to the changing forces of history and experience. We cannot merely claim that the rights we espouse came from a perfect God, from the immutable nature of human beings, or even from the logic of democracy or the commitment to equality. Rights cannot be discovered, since they are not waiting anywhere out there to be found. Nor can they be logically deduced from any external reality or constructed from arguments, since the premises on which any such deduction or construction must be based are themselves the product of differing experiences and perceptions. Rights must be invented by human beings, based on experience, especially our long collective experience with wrongs created by human beings. And they must be advocated in the marketplace of competing ideas.

If rights grow out of the experiences and histories of human beings, then they are more a function of nurture than of nature. The term "nurtural rights," though a bit clumsy, is closer to the truth than natural rights. In this respect, rights—like morals—are somewhat situational, not in the sense that there is no commonality in their application to differing situations, but in the sense that they reflect the differing histories and conditions in which people have found themselves when they have invented, articulated, and ranked rights.*

It should not be surprising, therefore, that I disagree with those who wrote the oft-quoted paragraph of our Declaration of Independence that invoked "the Laws of Nature and of Nature's God" as the source of their rights. The authors of the Declaration believed certain "truths" to "be self-evident," among them that human beings "are endowed by their Creator with certain unalienable Rights," and that "among these are Life, Liberty, and the pursuit of Happiness." The Declaration then moved from God-given natural law to man-made positive law based on social contract, by asserting that "to secure these rights, Governments are instituted among Men, deriving their just powers from the consent of the governed." In other words, the *substance* of our rights comes from outside our laws—from nature and nature's God. But the *process* by which these God-given rights (and presumably other rights of lower status) *become secured* is a positive-law, democratic process. Hence the shift from a natural-law declaration of our rights to a positive-law constitutionalization of these rights.

---

*In his concurring opinion in *Rasul v. Bush*, 542 U.S. _____ (2004), Justice Anthony Kennedy referred to the existence of an "ascending scale of rights" depending on an individual's connection to the United States. He was quoting Justice Robert Jackson, who said that in the United States, "The alien . . . has been accorded a generous and ascending scale of rights as he increases his identity with our society." *Johnson v. Eisentrager*, 339 U.S. 763 (1950), at p. 770.

There are many problems with this formulation. If the truths contained in these laws are so "self-evident," why did the British authorities, and American Tories, not recognize them? How are conflicts among self-evident truths to be resolved? What if there is a conflict between the law of "Nature's God," as understood by some elites, and "the consent of the governed"? From whom among the governed is consent required?

Consider, once again, the example of slavery, which many whites believed was consistent with the law of nature's God but which surely was inconsistent with equality, liberty, consent, and the "unalienable rights" of the enslaved, who were regarded as property rather than citizenry. Or consider why the right of the colonies to separate from Great Britain was granted by the "laws of Nature and Nature's God," while the same laws less than a century later denied the Confederate states the right to separate from the United States. And what about the rights of disbelievers, skeptics, and agnostics? From whom or from where do their rights derive—if they indeed have rights? Both former president George H. W. Bush and former presidential candidate Alan Keyes have suggested that atheists cannot be good citizens, since they do not accept the statement in the Declaration of Independence that Americans are endowed "by their Creator" with rights. Did God give human beings the right not to believe in Him?* If so, why do His ministers threaten eternal damnation for its exercise? Does the nature of human beings require belief in God? In a specific God? If so, which God? The Declaration of Independence does not answer these and other vexing questions raised by its deistic formulation of the source of rights. Although it invokes the laws of nature's God, it never mentions the Bible, Christianity, or organized religion.

---

*On his deathbed, the philosopher Sidney Morgenbesser asked a question that, in typical Jewish style, he answered with another question: "Why is God making me suffer so much? Just because I don't believe in him?" Douglas Martin, "Sidney Morgenbesser, 82, Kibitzing Philosopher, Dies," *New York Times*, August 4, 2004.

Jefferson, Franklin, and Paine, among others, had great doubts about organized religion but believed in a nonintervening God of nature. Thomas Paine was a radical anti-Christian who wrote a book trashing the Bible: *The Age of Reason.*

As a consensus-building document advocating a moral but extralegal course of action, the Declaration was written at a level of abstraction and generality designed not to offend anyone whose support was being elicited. It should not be misread as presenting a coherent—or authoritative—theory of the sources of our rights. Rather, it is part of the genre of political "midrash,"* akin to the religious midrashim of God giving Moses the Ten Commandments at Sinai, Allah dictating the Koran to an illiterate Muhammad, and Joseph Smith discovering the buried gold tablets in the New York countryside. Yet because it forms an important rhetorical basis for one of our central foundational documents, it is often cited as part of our positive law, especially by those who approve its invocation of a divine source of rights.[5]

A careful reading of the entire Declaration of Independence—not just its quotable rhetoric—lends considerable support, however, to an experiential approach to rights. The centerpiece of the Declaration is a catalog of wrongs—of "abuses and usurpations"—which made it the "right" of the Americans "to institute new Government" in order to provide "new Guards for their future security."** Thus the signatories of the Declaration invoked both the laws of nature and their own experience with injustice—with wrongs—to justify their demand for

---

*Midrashim (the plural of midrash) are interpretations of the biblical text by the use of illustrative stories, explanations, commentaries, and other forms of exegesis.

**"New Guards" certainly suggests newly invented rights that did not previously exist and are not eternal. In fact, many of these new guards were adopted as positive law in the Bill of Rights, several of which were enacted in direct response to the wrongs catalogued in the Declaration. See Alan Dershowitz, *America Declares Independence* (Hoboken, N.J.: Wiley, 2003) at pp. 116–118.

rights, to serve as guards against the recurrence of these wrongs. Their claims based on experience were, in my view, far more compelling than those based on God, nature, and other "self-evident"—but much disputed—propositions. As John Hart Ely has pointed out,

> The Declaration of Independence was, to put it bluntly, a brief (with certain features of an indictment). People writing briefs are likely, and often well advised, to throw in arguments of every hue. People writing briefs for revolution are obviously unlikely to have apparent positive law on their side, and are therefore well advised to rely on natural law.[6]

This is a tactic with roots in antiquity. As Aristotle observed: "If the written law tells against our case, clearly we must appeal to the universal law."[7] The opposite is equally true: If natural law would undercut the authority of the lawmaker, then he will appeal to positive law. That is the nature of the harlot. She will go with anyone who wants to use her, but at a price. Thus, when our Constitution was drafted, only a few years after the Declaration, neither God nor nature was explicitly cited as the source of rights. Indeed, it was referred to at the time as "the Godless Constitution." Now that we were a nation of laws, the last thing the framers—now the lawmakers and enforcers—wanted was to encourage extra-legal actions based on vague notions of natural law. Natural law had served its purpose in the campaign for independence from Britain. It was no longer useful. The harlot had lost her charm, now that our nation had settled down and the positive law, whatever its limitations, was *our* positive law.

But changing experiences demanded a changing conception of rights, and thus a changing constitution. We had to fight a Civil War to undo the inferior status accorded blacks under our original constitution. The courts proved inadequate to the task of fulfilling the Declaration's false promise of equality. The post–Civil War amendments—

the Thirteenth, Fourteenth, and Fifteenth—created new rights based on old wrongs. The process continues to this day with Supreme Court decisions such as *Brown v. Board of Education* and legislation such as the civil rights laws.

Building a system of rights from the bottom up, based on the experiences of injustice, is consistent with the common-law approach to the development of legal doctrines. Injustice provides the occasion for change. The history of the common law has been a history of adapting legal doctrine to avoid or minimize injustice. When all parties to a dispute believe that justice has been done, there is no occasion for litigation, no need for dispute resolution, and hence no stimulus to change the law. The case reports are not about instances of perceived justice, but about injustices in search of remedies. Even Aristotle's theory of corrective justice recognized the close relationship between wrongs and the need for corrective laws to restore equilibrium.

The same is true of the history of rights. Where the majority does justice to the minority, there is little need for rights. But where injustice prevails, rights become essential. Wrongs provoke rights, as our checkered history confirms.

This rights-from-wrongs approach is also consistent with the scientific method of building new theory on the mistakes of past scientists. Richard P. Feynman once described an important value of science in the following terms:

> The scientist has a lot of experience with ignorance and doubt and uncertainty, and this experience is of very great importance, I think. When a scientist doesn't know the answer to a problem, he is ignorant. When he has a hunch as to what the result is, he is uncertain. And when he is pretty darn sure of what the result is going to be, he is still in some doubt. We have found it of paramount importance that in order to progress we must recognize our ignorance and leave

room for doubt. Scientific knowledge is a body of statements of varying degrees of certainty—some most unsure, some nearly sure, but none *absolutely* certain.

Now, we scientists are used to this, and we take it for granted that it is perfectly consistent to be unsure, that it is possible to live and *not* know. But I don't know whether everyone realizes this is true. Our freedom to doubt was born out of a struggle against authority in the early days of science. It was a very deep and strong struggle: permit us to question—to doubt—to not be sure.[8]

With regard to law as well, we will never achieve absolute certainty or perfect justice. And that is a good, not a bad, thing because it stimulates an eternal quest for better justice based on our past mistakes and our current uncertainties. Just as progress in science "comes from a satisfactory philosophy of ignorance,"[9] so too with rights: Progress in rights comes from a satisfactory theory of wrongs.

It is beyond the scope of this book to offer a complete and comprehensive new approach to precisely which rights are needed at a particular time and place. Its goal is to begin the work of constructing an approach that rests neither on the shadowy metaphysics of natural law nor the empty tautology of legal positivism. I recognize how much easier it is to attack the traditional schools than to construct and defend a new one. Perhaps it is impossible to come up with a completely unassailable theory of rights. If that were so, it would be an argument in favor of, not against, a process-oriented, advocacy approach to rights. Doing rights, while advocating a continuous process of right*ing*—of exploring the possible sources of rights outside of natural and positive law and inventing and implementing new rights as a work in progress—is entirely consistent with an acceptance of the possibility, indeed the likelihood, that we will never devise a perfect theory of rights. Advocating rights without a perfect theory is far better than silently accepting wrongs until a theory can be perfected.*

The development of rights is an ongoing human process, because changing experiences demonstrate the need for changing rights. Rights once "discovered" or "revealed" do not remain immutable. The process of "righting" must always adapt to the human capacity to do wrong. History proves that rights are not eternal and fixed. What was believed to be a right in one time and place was shown by experience to be a wrong. Hobbes, for example, listed among the "rights of sovereigns" the right to censor anything that was not "the truth."

> [I]t is annexed to the Sovereignty, to be Judge of what Opinions and Doctrines are averse, and what conducing to Peace; and consequently, on what occasions, how farre, and what, men are to be trusted withall, in speaking to Multitudes of people; and who shall examine the Doctrines of all bookes before they be published.[10]

Experience has shown that the "right" of a sovereign to censor produces grave wrongs and that to prevent these wrongs we should instead create a right not to be censored by government (except, perhaps, in extraordinary situations). That right is now recognized by American positive law as well as by most theories of natural law. Its source, however, is human experience with the wrongs of government censorship of precisely the kind that Hobbes believed was a right.

Slavery is another example. As I will document later, many Southern intellectuals believed not only that slave *owners* had a God-given right to own "human property," but that the slaves *themselves* had a right to be kept as "Christian slaves." No reasonable person would accept

---

*Kafka, in my estimation, makes a more powerful case for rights by portraying a dystopian world without them than do many positive advocates of rights who seek to demonstrate a utopian world, with rights.

such a "right" today. Instead, we have constructed a right to be a free laborer—a non-slave—from the experience with the wrongs of slavery. That right is today recognized by positive law as well as by all theories of natural law. It too is based not on some divine source—indeed the Bible justifies slavery—but rather on human experience. (So too with the right of laborers to form unions and bargain collectively.)

It is incontestable that rights change over time and place, but they do not change at a steady pace or in a symmetrical manner. Long periods of time pass with few or no changes in rights. Then, suddenly, there is a burgeoning of new rights. My late colleague Stephen Jay Gould observed a phenomenon in nature that he called "punctuated equilibrium," pursuant to which evolutionary changes "happen in fits and starts." Though I am generally wary of using scientific observations of natural phenomena as metaphors for human inventions, there are some striking similarities between Gould's observations about evolution and my observations about rights.* Gould's approach has been summarized as follows:

Darwin saw evolution as a slow, continuous process, without sudden jumps. However, if you study the fossils of organisms found in subsequent geological layers, you will see long intervals in which nothing changed ("equilibrium"), "punctuated" by short, revolutionary transition, in which species became extinct and replaced by wholly new forms. Instead of a slow, continuous progression, the evolution of life on Earth seems more like the life of a soldier: long periods of boredom interrupted by rare moments of terror.[11]

Cataclysmic natural events—such as large meteor strikes, sustained periods of unusual heat or cold, and massive volcanic eruptions—

---

*This is, perhaps, no accident since I taught a course with Gould and with Robert Nozick over several years in which we compared and contrasted the epistemologies of science, philosophy, and law.

kill off some entire species as well as the less adaptable within surviving species. These are nature's version of "wrongs," though nature—like the classically insane person—knows not right from wrong. Yet by quickly wiping out a large number of living things, nature accelerates the pace of evolution. This is not part of some grand plan to push lower forms of life into evolving in a particular direction—toward human consciousness or some other higher form of being. It simply is the nonintelligent, nonpurposive workings of natural forces that accidentally produce change. This change is seen as "progress" by those who benefit from it and who are capable of evaluating it, namely, human beings. Nature does not seek progress or regress. It merely changes life in response to natural phenomena, and it changes it at no preordained or deliberate rate of speed, but rather in response to the fits and starts of other natural events.*

Though human inventions such as rights, and the wrongs that stimulate them, are neither as unintelligent nor as purposeless as natural changes, they too seem "to happen in fits and starts." The history of rights shows long periods during which few changes seem to occur. Then a grievous human wrong, like the Holocaust, suddenly takes place. The world eventually acknowledges the wrong and responds with a burgeoning of rights, as occurred following the Second World War, when international human rights took giant steps forward.[12] Sometimes the wrong is not sudden, but rather of long duration, such as slavery. It is the recognition of the wrong—or its defeat after a conflict—that serves as a stimulus for the development of the right. The post–Civil War constitutional amendments quickly turned a right to own slaves into a right not to be owned as a slave.

There are numerous historical examples of rights burgeoning immediately after the acknowledgment of grievous wrongs,** though

---

*This is not to suggest that nature is not ordered or determined by certain rules, but only that it is not directed by any purpose or externally imposed goals.

this has certainly not always been the case.[13] There have also been some historical examples of rights quickly contracting in the aftermath of wrongs that were believed to be caused by excessive rights.[14] We may experience such a contraction in response to the terrorist attacks of recent years, and the contraction may become more extreme and widespread if terrorism were to escalate.[15]

An example of this complex phenomenon at work is provided by the American response to the Japanese attack on Pearl Harbor. Immediately after that day of "infamy," a liberal American administration[16] ordered the confinement of more than 100,000 Americans of Japanese descent in detention centers, where most remained for several years. The Supreme Court, with the concurrence of several liberal justices, approved this massive violation of rights. Within a few years after the end of the war, many Americans came to see this race-based detention as a grievous wrong, never to be repeated. Our government officially apologized to the detainees and paid them token compensation.

When the World Trade Center and the Pentagon were attacked by Muslim extremists, most of whom were of the Wahhabi sect from Saudi Arabia, no government official even suggested a roundup of all Muslims, Saudis, or Wahhabis comparable to the Japanese detention. It had become an American consensus that despite the Supreme Court decision approving the roundup, it was wrong. To do anything similar to Muslims, Saudis, or Wahhabis would violate their rights. There is now an accepted right in America not to be confined on the basis of race, religion, or national origin. This right did not grow out of any positive or natural law—these did not fundamentally change within a generation—but rather out of our expe-

---

**For example, the United Nations was founded soon after the end of World War II, and its Universal Declaration of Human Rights was drafted a few years after that. Important new rights also followed World War I, with its use of mustard gas and other new wrongs.

rience with the wrongs of the Japanese detention.[17] Thus, within a relatively short period of time, one cataclysmic event, the Japanese attack on Pearl Harbor, produced a dramatic contraction of rights. Then another terrible wrong, the mass detention that followed, produced a recognition of the right not to be confined solely on the basis of race or national origin, even during national emergencies.

The righting process is always in flux. Its pace will change with the human capacity to inflict wrongs. It is a never-ending process that rarely produces a static result or a perfect set of eternal rights. We must strive not for perfection but for pragmatic rights that are capable of keeping up with the human capacity to generate new and more horrible wrongs.

II *Some Challenges to*
    Experience as the Source
    of Rights

't both be right"—to which the rabbi responded, "You too
t." The husband and wife can both be right—and wrong.
nore complex and nuanced than language. There may be
e "rights" in any situation, and they will sometimes conflict.
he Brothers Karamazov, Fyodor Dostoyevsky posed a wonder-
ral dilemma to which there is plainly no single right answer.
il, a highly regarded town official who is married and has
en, confides in Zozima that fourteen years earlier he killed a
n in a well-planned act motivated by jealousy. The peasant
was suspected of the crime died before he could be brought to
No one would materially benefit from Mikhail's belated con-
on, but his innocent wife—whom he married after the killing—
his young children would suffer grievously: "My wife may die of
"; "My children, even if they are not stripped of rank and prop-
, will become a convict's children, and that forever"; "And what
emory I shall leave in their hearts." Mikhail and Zozima cite con-
ting scriptural and philosophical sources in support of confess-
or remaining silent.

If he could join this debate, Kant would surely argue that truth is
that matters, regardless of the consequences. Jeremy Bentham
ould point to the accumulated unhappiness that would result
om a selfish confession—selfish because, according to Dos-
oyevsky, it would be designed to bring salvation to Mikhail's con-
cience at a high cost to his family. Other philosophers would invoke
principles pointing in different directions, some arguing that consequentialist thinking would produce great evils in other cases (e.g.,
killing a "worthless" witness in order to spare innocent family members the grief of their breadwinner's being caught), with others arguing that suffering in silence or even suicide would be a more
noble and moral act for Mikhail than shaming his family to assure
himself paradise. The question is not which of these solutions—or
others—is preferable. The question is whether there is only one

CHAPTER 9

Is There Always a Right A

they can
are righ
Life is
multipl
In T
ful mo
Mikha
childr
woma
who
trial.
fessi
and
grie
erty
a m
flic
ing

al
w
f
t
s

I F RIGHTS ARE experiential and ch
than natural and unalienable, what happ
clash? For those who believe in the inerrancy and
natural law, both sides of a moral- or right-based ar
be right.* But in real life there may indeed be both a r
a right to choose, just as there may be a right to life a
self-defense. Why is it supposed that rights may not be i
conflict?[1] This conflict may require an agreed-upon
reaching a workable resolution within a pluralistic dem

An old story about a wise Eastern European rabbinic
lustrates this reality. The rabbi was hearing a dispute betw
tranged husband and wife. The wife argued that her hus
violated her marital rights by sleeping with other women a
ing to give her enough money for necessities. The rabbi liste
ruled, "You are right, my daughter." Then he heard her hu
claim that his marital rights had been violated by his wife's ref
sleep with him and to cook his meals. The rabbi listened and
"You are right, my son." The rabbi's student interjected, "But, r

---

*Ronald Dworkin supposes that "there is often a single right answer to complex q
tions of law and political morality." See Taking Rights Seriously (Cambridge, M
Harvard University Press, 1977), p. 279. But surely many such questions have mu
ple right and wrong answers.

right solution, and if so, what is its authoritative source and how shall we deal with powerful and persuasive counterarguments? I believe that reasonable people—moral, religious, and good—can and should disagree about this and other complex moral conundrums and that we should not presume there is a single, perfect answer to be discovered if only we could access the proper source.

Another example, inspired by Dostoyevsky's Grand Inquisitor scene, also tests the principle that truth is absolute. Imagine being on a visit to the Qumran caves outside Jerusalem and coming upon a previously undiscovered Dead Sea scroll, much older than the ones from the time of Jesus, that contains the account of a meeting of religious leaders deciding how to deal with rampant disbelief, lawlessness, and violence. They come up with the idea to stage a "revelation" on a mountain called Sinai from which God will "give" ten commandments carved on two tablets. They argue about the content of the commandments and finally compromise on the ones we know. The scroll contains considerable details about the staging necessary to persuade the common folk that the revelation is genuine. A later scroll, also newly found, suggests the staging of a crucifixion and resurrection of a man who they will claim was God's son. Someone suggests that he be born to a virgin, as is common in Greek mythology, and that he be crucified and then miraculously resurrected. Calvary is selected as the site for this final miracle. Other scrolls could contain similar staged miracles involving Muhammad and Joseph Smith.

I mean no disrespect by these made-up scenarios; they are merely designed to test principles. You, the finder of the scroll, are a deeply religious person, equally committed to truth. You also believe that organized religions, particularly the Judeo-Christian faiths, are extremely valuable and central to the lives of millions, including your own parents and grandparents, whose faith would be shaken by the disclosure of your findings. You are convinced beyond any doubt that the scrolls are authentic and that the events reported by the Gospels or other holy books were completely fabricated by people of utter goodwill—they were truly "pious frauds." Do you disclose your findings? Remain silent? Destroy the scrolls?

A more mundane variation on this unrealistic scenario occurs whenever a religious leader—on the eve of delivering a major sermon on the importance of believing in God—suddenly begins to doubt God's existence. This surely happened to many rabbis, priests, and ministers during the Holocaust. Does truth require cancellation of the sermon, revelation of the new belief, change in tone, or simply a crossing of one's fingers as the original sermon is delivered?

These are daunting questions—and there are many others—to which a single correct answer would be insulting to the complexity and diversity of the human mind and experience. It is the brilliance of great literature that it is never satisfied with a single, correct answer to a complex and often ambiguous human dilemma. Its characters—through their internal dialogues as well as their external conflicts—reflect the diversity of human experiences and emotions. A great moral philosopher must have the insights of a poet.

Even schematic hypothetical situations—carefully crafted for their one-dimensional simplicity—defy singular answers. The famous "trolley track" dilemmas are designed to show there is no right answer: You are a trolley conductor whose brakes have failed. You see a fork in the tracks ahead. If you turn right, your trolley will hit a group of children; if you turn left, you will hit a single old drunk; if you fail to choose, random forces will choose for you. A complicating variation has a straight track leading directly to the children, but there is a turn you could take that would lead you to the drunk. Under this variation, if you do nothing, the children die. You must actively choose to kill the drunk. Countless variations on these "tragic choice" dilemmas are imaginable.[2] Each has multiple "right" and "wrong" answers.

The difficult issue—of morality, legality, and practicality—is how to devise an acceptable process for resolving such conflicts in a pluralistic democracy committed to balancing the preferences of the majority against the rights of minorities. There can be no absolutely perfect resolution to these conflicts.[3] They reflect deeply felt moral concerns, intuitions, historical experiences, and worldviews that may and do differ over times and cultures. Recall that as recently as two centuries ago—a blip on the time line of recorded history—most thoughtful and decent people honestly believed in the moral inequality of whites and blacks, men and women, Christians and "heathens," heterosexuals and homosexuals, as well as other dualities. Who can know which of our contemporary moral beliefs—for example, the distinction between the value of human and animal life—will seem unacceptable to our progeny in generations to come?

Law, morality, and even truth are ongoing processes for resolving conflicts in a democracy comprising people with different histories, experiences, perceptions, value hierarchies, and worldviews. To expect one "correct" or one "true" moral answer to emerge from such different backgrounds is to devalue our diversity. We respect our heterogeneity when we construct democratic processes for compromise and for accommodating and living with the inevitable differences—even about rights—that are inherent in such a diverse society.

It should not be surprising that the United States has served as the great laboratory for constructing these conflict-accommodating processes, since our population is the most diverse in the history of the world. We began as a community of immigrants and dissenters with a relatively narrow range of ethnic backgrounds. By the end of the nineteenth century, these backgrounds had diversified, along with our religious differences. Unlike some other countries, which share a more unified tradition with regard to the substance of morality, law, and rights,[4] we have developed a consensus about the processes for resolving our substantive differences. Our system of checks and balances may often result in deadlock or only gradual change, but it is a system designed to accommodate differences. Compromise has been the essence of the American experience, even in areas as difficult to compromise as family conflict and religion.[5]

A recent case decided by the Supreme Court illustrates how we tend to resolve intractable moral conflicts by resorting to process and procedure.[6] The case pitted the rights of the parents of two young children against the rights of the children's grandparents. A woman named Tommie and a man named Brad had two children. They never married and eventually separated. Brad moved in with his parents and brought his children to their home for weekend visits. Two years later Brad died and Tommie married Kelly, who then adopted Tommie's two children. The children's paternal grandparents—the late Brad's father and mother—wanted to keep seeing their grandchildren on a regular basis (two weekends per month and two weeks during the summer), but the parents wanted them to have less time together (one daytime visit per month). The Washington State statute empowered the courts to order whatever visitation rights would serve "the best interests" of the children, without regard to the wishes of the parents. Pursuant to that statute, a lower court judge granted the grandparents' petition for broad visitation rights, citing his own familial experiences: "I look back on some personal experiences. . . . We always spen[t] as kids a week with one set of grandparents and another set of grandparents, [and] it happened to work out in our family that [it] turned out to be an enjoyable experience. Maybe that can, in this family, if that is how it works out."

The Supreme Court of Washington reversed that ruling and struck down that law on the ground that it "unconstitutionally interferes with the fundamental rights of parents to rear their children."

The stage was thus set for petitioning the United States Supreme Court to resolve this conflict of alleged rights: those of the parents (in this case one biological, one adoptive) against those of the grandparents (both biological, through the dead natural father).

There is not a word, syllable, suggestion, or innuendo in the Constitution that controls, or even informs, this conflict. Nor were there any binding constitutional precedents or history on this point. The high court has, of course, talked about "parental rights" in relation to the state, the schools, and other outside institutions, but not in relation to grandparents who also claim some parental or family rights. Reasonable people can and should disagree—as a matter of policy—on what the correct answer is. The Washington legislature, presumably after considering all sides of this issue, came down in favor of limited grandparental rights, as forty-seven other states have also done. That should resolve the question as a matter of constitutional law. Where there is no constitutional prohibition on a particular answer and when a state legislature acts reasonably in arriving at an answer, the Supreme Court has no business second-guessing the state's answer. Only an unreconstructed judicial activist—a judge who believes in substituting his own personal moral philosophy for that of duly elected legislators—would consider striking down the Washington statute, or the statute of another state that came to the opposite conclusion and prohibited grandparents from visiting grandchildren over the objection of parents. Supreme Court Justice Louis Brandeis, a paragon of judicial restraint, understood that states must be accorded considerable flexibility so that they can be "laboratories" of social experimentation. States should be free to come to differing conclusions on divisive and controversial moral and psychological issues not governed by the Constitution, so long as they do so in a reasonable manner. Did the Washington State statute meet this criterion? That is the question addressed by the justices.

The Supreme Court began its analysis by looking to experience:

The demographic changes of the past century make it difficult to speak of an average American family. The composition of families varies greatly from household to household. While many children may have two married parents and grandparents who visit regularly, many other children are raised in single-parent households. In 1996, children living with only one parent accounted for 28 percent of all children under age 18 in the United States. . . . Understandably, in these single-parent households, persons outside the nuclear family are called upon with increasing frequency to assist in the everyday tasks of child rearing. In many cases, grandparents play an important role. For example, in 1998, approximately 4 million children—or 5.6 percent of all children under age 18—lived in the household of their grandparents.

The nationwide enactment of nonparental visitation statutes is assuredly due, in some part, to the States' recognition of these changing realities of the American family. Because grandparents and other relatives undertake duties of a parental nature in many households, States have sought to ensure the welfare of the children therein by protecting the relationships those children form with such third parties.

Despite this experiential basis for allowing grandparental visitation to be ordered by the courts, a plurality of the U.S. Supreme Court struck down the Washington statute on the ground that it was too broad and open-ended. The court also cited experience to challenge any ideal conception of child rearing:

In an ideal world, parents might always seek to cultivate the bonds between grandparents and their grandchildren. Needless to say, however, our world is far from perfect, and in it the decision whether such an intergenerational relationship would be beneficial in any specific case is for the parent to make in the first instance. And, if a fit parent's decision of the kind at issue here becomes subject to judicial review, the court must accord at least some special weight to the parent's own determination.

Because the Washington statute did not accord sufficient deference to the wishes of the custodial parents and because it authorized "any person"—not only grandparents—to petition for visitation, it was held unconstitutional. The high court thus evaded the direct clash of morality between claims of parents and grandparents and decided the case on technical legal issues, leaving open the question of whether a narrowly tailored law granting some visitation rights to grandparents, over the objection of parents, would be upheld.

The most interesting opinion in the case was written by Justice Scalia, who personally believes that only parents have a God-given natural right to raise their children.

In my view, a right of parents to direct the upbringing of their children is among the "unalienable Rights" with which the Declaration of Independence proclaims "all Men . . . are endowed by their Creator."

But Scalia also believes that,

The Declaration of Independence, however, is not a legal prescription conferring powers upon the courts. . . . Consequently, while I would think it entirely compatible with the commitment to representative democracy set forth in the founding documents to argue, in legislative chambers or in electoral campaigns, that the state has no power to interfere with parents' authority over the rearing of their children, I do not believe that the power which the Constitution confers upon me as a judge entitles me to deny legal effect to laws that (in my view) infringe upon what is (in my view) [an] unenumerated [unalienable] right.

One can quarrel with Justice Scalia's personal belief that parents have a God-given unalienable right to prevent grandparents from visiting their grandchildren, even when such visits are in the grandchildren's best interest. I would certainly want to know where such a right comes from and why grandparents do not have a countervailing right to at least some visitation. But it is difficult to quarrel with his legal conclusion that if the Constitution does not accord parents this exclusive right, the state retains the power to strike an appropriate balance, so long as it legislates in a reasonable manner.

When I was a child, I once asked my father why the mezuzah—the religious object that adorns the doorpost of a Jewish home—is always placed on a slant. My father asked our rabbi, who explained: "There were two schools of thought: One believed that it should be placed horizontally, the other vertically. Each was convinced it was correct but could not persuade the other. Finally, they split the difference by agreeing that it should be placed at a slant halfway between horizontal and vertical." What a wonderful symbol for a home, where compromise is always required. It is also a symbol for how America, at its best, has sometimes compromised and avoided the religious and political polemicism of other nations.

We should not strive for the uniformity of one absolutely correct morality, truth, or justice.* The active and never-ending processes of moralizing, truth searching, and justice seeking are far superior to the passive acceptance of one truth. The right*ing* process, like the truth*ing* process, is ongoing. Indeed, there are dangers implicit in

---

*I am not speaking of scientific truth, which may well be singular and uniform (though always subject to challenge and reformulation), but rather of moral truth, which is not nearly as objective.

accepting—and acting upon—any single philosophy of morality. Conflicting moralities serve as checks against the tyranny of singular truth. I would not want to live in a world in which Jeremy Bentham's or even John Stuart Mill's utilitarianism reigned supreme to the exclusion of all Kantian and neo-Kantian approaches; nor would I want to live in an entirely Kantian world in which categorical imperatives were always slavishly followed. Bentham serves as a check on Kant and vice versa, just as religion serves as a check on science, science on religion, socialism on capitalism, capitalism on socialism.* Rights serve as a check on democracy, and democracy serves as a check on rights.

Our constitutional system of checks and balances has an analogue in the marketplace of ideas. We have experienced the disasters produced by singular truths, whether religious, political, ideological, or economic. Those who believe they have discovered the ultimate truth tend to be less tolerant of dissent. As Hobbes put it: "Nothing ought to be regarded but the truth," and it "belongeth therefore to [the sovereign] to be judge" as to that truth. Put more colloquially, who needs differing—false—views when you have the one true view? Experience demonstrates we all do! The physicist Richard Feynman understood the lessons of human experience and the limitations of human knowledge far better than the philosopher Thomas Hobbes, as Feynman showed when he emphasized the basic "freedom to doubt"—a freedom that was born out of the "struggle against authority in the early days of science." That struggle persists.

---

*The eugenics movement, popular in the 1920s, illustrates this phenomenon. Religion served as a check on the excessive zeal of some advocates of human eugenics (such as Oliver Wendell Holmes Jr.). Then the Nazis' misuse of eugenics provided an experiential basis for opposing it.

If Rights Do Not Come from God or Nature, How Are They Different from Mere Preferences?

IF RIGHTS DO not come from "the laws of nature and of nature's God" and if they are not self-evident, then what gives certain personal preferences the special status of "rights"? Surely the answer cannot simply be that a given individual feels strongly enough about it. This would make the concept of rights entirely subjective and would rob it of all meaning.

In the first chapter of this book, I defined rights in a general way as something more enduring, more entrenched, more historically rooted, and more institutional than a mere majoritarian preference. In this chapter, I try to provide more affirmative experience-based criteria for distinguishing rights from preferences.

For positivists the distinction is relatively simple. Those preferences, and only those that are entrenched in the law as rights, are to be accorded that status. But this reductionistic formulation tells us nothing about which preferences *ought* to be so entrenched. For advocates of divine natural law, the answer is only a bit more complex: A right is anything God has decided is a right. Discerning God's intention, however, may be somewhat problematic. For biblical fundamentalists, that intent is manifested in the text of various holy books. In this respect, these fundamentalists are close—at least structurally—to some legal positivists, with the former looking to the Bible and the latter looking to secular law books.

The secular natural-law advocates have a heavier burden in distinguishing rights from strongly held preferences. They must derive rights from some combination of human nature and reason. Or they must construct rights from the raw material of first principles, such as equality, fairness, or liberty. In this respect, they are not much different from some nonfundamentalist religious advocates of natural law and natural rights, since those sources are equally ethereal and subjective.

Contemporary Catholic thinkers, who reject both biblical fundamentalism and legal positivism, have contributed a brilliant, if not always entirely satisfying, literature to the debate over natural law and natural rights.[1] Like Jewish and Muslim nonfundamentalists, they have designed institutional processes for interpreting biblical texts. These processes—referred to as "reading the Bible within the church," or "Halakah" (the Road) or "Shari'ah" (the Broad Path)— are akin to secular common law, with authoritative interpreters. In the end, the preferences these religious interpreters choose to call rights (or obligations, or moral truths) often seem to reflect result-oriented thinking that generally comes out in favor of preordained doctrinal or political positions. For example, the sacred texts of virtually all religions can support—and have been interpreted to support—completely opposing views on capital punishment, abortion, gay rights, preemptive war, even terrorism.[2]

Lawyers and legal scholars, especially good ones, are experts at result-oriented advocacy. They shift the level of analysis of a question so that the answer comes out the way they want it to. Like a good chess player, a clever advocate always thinks several moves ahead. If an abstract, rights-based, Kantian analysis will eventually lead to the conclusion sought by the advocate, he will frame the question so that it is amenable to that sort of analysis. If a more utilitarian analysis will bring him where he wants to go, he will frame the question in that manner and then invoke either act or rule utilitarianism,[3] depending on which is more likely to lead him to his desired outcome. Philosophy as a cover for politics is as old as Socrates and Plato. And God as a justifier of wrongs predates the Torah.

There is a practical benefit to maintaining conflicting, even incompatible, theories of rights. Conflicting theories serve as a check on each other and on the tendency toward taking any one theory to dangerous logical extremes. Experience has shown that singular philosophies—those that insist that they alone reflect "truth" and that all others are "false"—produce grievous wrongs, especially if they gain the power to suppress "false" ideas. As Richard Feynman once observed:

> We are at the very beginning of time for the human race. It is not unreasonable that we grapple with problems. But there are tens of thousands of years in the future. Our responsibility is to do what we can, learn what we can, improve the solutions, and pass them on. It is our responsibility to leave the people of the future a free hand. In the impetuous youth of humanity, we can make grave errors that can stunt our growth for a long time. This we will do if we say we have the answers now, so young and ignorant as we are. If we suppress all discussion, all criticism, proclaiming "This is the answer, my friends; man is saved!" we will doom humanity for a long time to the chains of authority, confined to the limits of our present imagination. It has been done so many times before.
>
> It is our responsibility as scientists, knowing the great progress which comes from a satisfactory philosophy of ignorance, the great progress which is the fruit of freedom of thought, to proclaim the value of this freedom; to teach how doubt is not to be feared but welcomed and discussed; and to demand this freedom as our duty to all coming generations.[4]

I seek to enter my approach to the sources of rights in a democracy as one of these competing truths in the marketplace of ideas. If experience with wrongs is the source of our rights, then a right is a restriction on governmental power that history has proved necessary for preventing (or slowing down) the recurrence of governmentally authorized wrongs that occurred because of the absence of such a restriction. Rights, thus defined, will expand, contract, and change over time, though more slowly and deliberately than mere preferences. They will also have to be continually defended and explained by reference to our ever-changing experiences.

In this respect the difference between a strongly held preference and a right is not absolute or natural. It is very much a matter of degree, based on changing historical experiences with wrongs. In this book I try to defend my strong preference for a society based on fundamental rights. That is all I can do—defend my *preference* for *rights*. I argue that based on our experiences over time, we should prefer to live in a society in which the government is denied certain powers, such as the power to censor even deeply offensive speech, or the power to restrict or promote religion. I also argue that we should all prefer to live in a society in which no citizen can be imprisoned, executed, deported, or otherwise deprived of basic freedoms without "due process of law." Finally, I argue that we should all prefer to live in a society where all people are deemed equal and are treated as equals by the government.

A society that recognizes and enforces certain basic rights—including uncensored expression, freedom of conscience, due process, democracy, and equal protection of the laws—is preferable to a society that does not. That is my case for rights. That is why I would leave, if I could, any society that did not protect rights in general and these rights in particular, believing as I do that the right to leave an oppressive country and settle elsewhere is among the most basic of rights.[5] If I could not leave, I would be willing to fight, perhaps even die, for these fundamental rights. But I make no claim for these rights beyond my ability to persuade you that history has shown them to be important enough to be given a special status in the hierarchy of preferences. There is no natural or divine line separating rights from strongly held preferences. Rights are fundamental limitations on state power that should be accepted by those who govern and those who are governed on the basis of human experience. Their authority may be explicit, as in a written constitution, or implicit, as an unwritten consensus developed over time.

If rights have no authority beyond some kind of social or political agreement, what distinguishes rights from preferences? That is a profound question that is rarely answered honestly. I try to answer it here by pointing to the history of wrongs.

I agree with Dworkin and others that individual rights should serve as trumps against the power of the state, but these trumps must be consistently advocated, not merely discovered or discerned. My approach is more activist in regard to rights. It requires constant reassessment and recommitment. It is less confident that others will simply recognize the eternal logical truth of its premises and conclusions.

The major conceptual difference between Dworkin's approach and mine is that his methodology is largely deductive: He reasons logically from the premises of the liberal, egalitarian, democratic state and deduces certain rights that naturally follow from the premises that a government must treat all of its citizens with equal concern and respect. My methodology is largely inductive: I look around at the experiences of people and nations over time and place—especially the experiences of injustice—and try to persuade others that, based on these experiences, people should conclude that entrenching certain rights into the positive law will, in the long run, produce a less unjust society.* The content of these rights will inevitably change over time with our experiences with new wrongs. I am confident that certain basic rights—such as freedom of conscience, expression, and religion—will endure. Others, which today seem essential, may prove unworthy of being trumps on majority preferences, while still others, which are not now recognized as rights, may achieve that status with changing experiences. This, too, parallels the progress of science. Certain basic principles—such as Newton's laws of motion—will probably endure over time, while other scientific "truths" that are accepted today will be disproved or modified by experience.

I reject Dworkin's view that the "rights" of the minority should trump the will of the majority "even if this would not be in the general interest," broadly defined and extended over time. Unless the community "will be better off in the long run as a whole"[6] by entrenching certain rights, it will be impossible to persuade people to do so, and my advocacy will fail—as it should in a democracy. My approach requires advocates of rights to persuade others by a variety of arguments—self-interest, doing the right thing, being consistent, adhering to one's own expressed values—that a system that entrenches and vindicates certain fundamental rights is preferable to one that does not. We will often fail in this effort, because the case for the long-term benefit of rights is a difficult one to make in a world in which short-term advantage is easier to see and understand. But this is an argument in favor of, not opposed to, the approach of continuous and persistent advocacy of inconvenient rights in a world impatient to get where it wants to go without the interference of countermajoritarian impediments, which inevitably slow down the progress of the will of the majority.

---

*Even this distinction is not as sharp as it may appear. Dworkin, too, ranks rights by reference to what we understand "from our general knowledge of society." Ronald Dworkin, *Taking Rights Seriously* (Cambridge, Mass.: Harvard University Press, 1977), p. 277.

At bottom, the ultimate source for Dworkin's nonpositivist rights is the fierce logic of his brilliant argumentation. He seems to believe that he can persuade the world that the very logic of the liberal, egalitarian, democratic state demands a system of rights outside of the law and transcending—trumping—the power of the state. Accepting his source of rights requires one to accept the brilliance of his logic (or some hidden metaphysical truth) rather than being persuaded that experience demonstrates the utility (broadly defined) of rights. He has succeeded in persuading me, and many others, as to much of his reasoning and many of his conclusions. But what about those whom he fails to persuade? Are they all necessarily wrong? Is there really only one right answer? And must it be Dworkin's? I might be happy if that were the case, but I must acknowledge that there are other reasonable positions that do not require complete acceptance of Dworkin's rigorous logic. The life of the law, as well as of morality, is, after all, experience, not logic—not even Dworkin's powerful and persuasive logic. And experience, unlike logic, rarely points inexorably toward a singular truth. It is the virtue, as well as the limitation, of logic that it points unerringly in one direction (if its original premises are accepted). It is the vice, as well as the richness, of experience that it may be perceived differently by different human beings with different backgrounds, value systems, and types of intelligence.[7] Experience is truly in the eye of the beholder.

That is why the experiential approach is somewhat more democratic and less elitist than Dworkin's: because it depends on continuing advocacy and it acknowledges that it may be rational and moral for a citizen to stick to his or her differing viewpoint, as distinguished from Dworkin's assertion that logic leads to only one rational and natural conclusion, regardless of the experiences, values, and intelligence of the particular person. While Dworkin relies on abstract and often technical philosophical analyses designed to persuade the academically oriented, the experiential approach relies on commonsense arguments growing out of the experiences of the people and an assessment of what will lead to a better society for them and others.

I often wish there were natural rights that could be invoked as external trumps, or that there was a natural and eternal line between rights and preferences. How much easier it would be to call upon God, nature, reason, a categorical imperative, a mythical social contract, a heuristic original position, or some inexorable Dworkinian logic in support of a preference for a legal system that recognizes the right to free speech. But to do so would not be faithful to my belief system or experiences. Jeremy Bentham once quipped that people invoke natural rights "when they wish to get their way without having to argue for it."[8] To which I would add "and without having to persuade a majority." Invoking God or nature is an argument stopper. "Because God says so." Or "because nature mandates." The ace of trumps. End of argument. Well, I have to argue for rights. All I can do is continue to advocate the right of free speech, based on the comparative experiences of nations that have accepted or rejected this risky and uncomfortable approach to governance. Rights come from the human experiences of injustice in societies without basic rights. The source of rights is, in a word, wrongs.

In one respect, the very question "Where do rights come from?" assumes an erroneous conclusion. To ask about the source of rights is to assume that such a source actually exists. Implicit in this assumption is yet another: that the source of any right (or rights-based system) is outside the structure of the humanly constructed legal system. Under my approach, the "source" of rights is in the experiences of humankind, most particularly our experiences with injustice. Yet it is somewhat imprecise to characterize our history of injustice as the "source" of our rights. The word *source* generally carries a somewhat different connotation. An analogy from biology might help to clarify the way in which I am using *source*. It can perhaps be said that the source of antibodies is infection. In one sense that may be true, but it is an incomplete account. Similarly, it is somewhat imprecise to say that the history of injustice caused by the merger of church and state is the source of the right to the free exercise of religion. This experience may be the *stimulus* for that right, but the *source* is the human ability to learn from experience and to entrench rights in our laws and in our consciousness. It is in that composite sense—experiential stimulus plus human reaction—that I use the term *source* in this discussion. This raises the question of whether my theory of rights is really more a sociological or anthropological (that is, descriptive) theory or a philosophical (that is, normative) theory.

CHAPTER 11

Does the Experiential Approach Confuse Philosophy with Sociology?

T HERE IS, OF course, a difference between a *philosophy* of rights on the one hand and an *anthropology* or *sociology* of rights on the other, though the difference may not be as sharp as advocates of natural law believe. One is in the nature of a moral inquiry, while the other is an empirical search. It can be argued that the approach to rights proposed in this book, being experiential and nurtural, is more akin to sociology than philosophy. But that would misunderstand what I am trying to do.

I am not seeking a merely descriptive approach to rights. I strongly believe that rights must have a moral component. Though I reject the notion that rights come directly from nature, I also reject the view that they come exclusively from nurture, without the mediation of morality. Empiricism informs morality but does not define it. Nature and nurture both have a vote, but neither has a veto, on the moral component of rights. Even the most stringent legal positivists acknowledge a close historical connection between legal rights and morality: As H. L. A. Hart observed, "the development of legal systems had been powerfully influenced by moral opinion, and, conversely, . . . moral standards had been profoundly influenced by law, so that the content of many legal rules mirrored moral rules or principles."[1] Even Oliver Wendell Holmes Jr., the author of the "bad man" theory of law,* recognized that "The law is the witness and external deposit of our moral life."[2]

A right that flies in the face of nature or scientific knowledge—for example, the right to smoke in crowded theaters—will simply not endure. Nor will a right that undercuts the experiences of a people, such as the right to bear arms in postwar Japan or to teach Holocaust denial in postwar Germany. But just as nature alone does not automatically translate into rights, experiences alone do not and should not dictate the content of rights. Rights come from a complex interaction of factors.

The one aspect of rights that must necessarily be governed by experience and empiricism is the evaluation of how effectively rights are working to achieve their stated goals. In order to persuade a democratic citizenry to accept any particular rights as a trump on the current will of the majority, an advocate must be able to demonstrate that a world (or a nation, or some other unit of democracy) will be a better place with this right than without it. Rights are not self-justifying (or "self-evident"). Nor can they be justified by logic alone. They need to work!—to accomplish something!—for the presumption of majority rule to be overcome. Evaluating the success or failure of a regime of rights is largely, though not entirely, an empirical undertaking: Agreeing on the ends sought to be served by rights is a moral enterprise (informed by experience), while deciding whether those ends have been achieved—and at what cost—is an empirical undertaking. And a major source for moral-empirical advocacy will be the experiences of people over time, especially their experiences with injustice.

---

*"If you want to know the law and nothing else, you must look at it as a bad man, who cares only for the material consequences which such knowledge enables him to predict, not as a good one, who finds his reasons for conduct, whether inside the law, or outside of it, in the vaguer sanctions of conscience." Oliver Wendell Holmes Jr., "The Path of the Law," *Harvard Law Review,* 10 (1897), p. 459.

Deciding what is moral—what is right—rarely involves the simple discovery of eternal truths. It is an ongoing process of trial and error, evaluation and reevaluation, based on changing experiences. Morality is not static. Once discovered, it should not remain unchallenged. It is not enough to deduce it, discover it, and declare it. One must constantly defend it, reconsider it, redefine it, and be prepared to change it.

What appeared to be right based on the knowledge of the past may now, with newer information, appear to be wrong. Indeed, what *was* right for a previous generation may *be* wrong for current or future generations.

Morality uninformed by experience is likely to be so abstract as to be incapable of resolving complex dilemmas. This has been the case with Kant's abstract imperatives, which have failed the test of human experience over time. Experience unstructured by morality, on the other hand, is mere narrative. There must be a continuing interplay between morality and experience. Morality does not emerge full-blown from the mind of man or the word of God. Even the Ten Commandments grew out of the injustices experienced in Genesis.[3] Morality must be honed over time by constant testing against the shoals of experience, but experience alone cannot dictate morality. A subtle and complex relationship exists between what is and what ought to be. We cannot derive our moral standards entirely from the nature of human beings, but neither can we ignore human nature in formulating and evaluating our values. Constructing a moral system is neither an entirely deductive nor an entirely inductive enterprise. Not unlike much of science, it requires abstract thinking and concrete testing. For some, like Einstein, the imaginings seem to come first and the testing later. For others, like Darwin, the observations appear to precede the construction of a general theory.* For all,

---

*Even this is a matter of degree. Einstein's theories did not emerge, fully blown, from his imagination, and Darwin obviously had some idea of what he was looking for.

there is the constant interplay among imagination, observation, and confirmation. Another point of agreement between science and morality is that for both, all conclusions must be tested against the realities of experience.

It does not confuse philosophy with sociology, normative with empirical, or deductive with inductive to acknowledge the interrelationship between the "ought" of morality and the "is" of experience. The difficult task is to assign each its proper weight in the process of constructing and evaluating a moral system.

An early historical example of the creative interplay between nature and morality is the biblical command to build cities of refuge for the accidental killer. The authors of the Bible certainly understood the inherent human impulse for vengeance. In one of the most subtle and innovative chapters of the Bible, God commands Moses to "appoint . . . cities of refuge . . . that the manslayer who killed any person *by accident* may flee into."[4] Willful murderers were not entitled to such refuge from the "blood avenger," but accidental killers were entitled to protection until passions cooled. The Bible recognized that the passion for revenge may be just as great against the accidental killer as against the premeditated murderer. To the dead victim's family, there may be little difference. Their loved one is dead, and the person who caused his death is guilty and deserves to die.[5] The writers of the Bible understood this human reality, but they also insisted that to understand is not necessarily to justify. The Bible seeks to protect the less culpable killer from the understandable passions of the blood avenger by allowing the killer to seek refuge in a designated place for a specified period of time. If the killer leaves the city of refuge and the blood avenger "finds him" and slays him, "there shall be no blood-guilt upon him," because an avenger who kills "while his heart is hot" is not as culpable as one who kills in cold blood.[6]

Simply allowing the natural inclination toward vengeance to take its course would—did—produce wrongs, including the revenge murders of morally innocent killers.[7] Ignoring the natural inclination toward vengeance is unrealistic. So the Bible channels this natural impulse by separating the accidental killer from the potential avenger until blood has cooled. Here we have an example of experience and logic working together to produce a reasonable resolution to an ancient conflict between natural vengeance and nurtural morality.

Among the most innovative and influential modern thinkers about the proper role of empiricism in the construction and evaluation of morality—especially in the context of law—was the French sociologist Émile Durkheim, who wrote in the late nineteenth and early twentieth centuries. Durkheim saw an intimate connection among empiricism, law, and morality. For him, the law was both the embodiment and the most accurate reflection of the morality of any given society. He believed that any claim for the universality of morality—or rights or law or any other social institution—would have to be proved empirically.[8] That is a descriptive claim: namely, that a certain morality or right *is* accepted by all, most, or some cultures. It is possible, of course, to make a claim about the universality of morality or rights that is entirely normative: namely, that a certain universal morality or right is the only just way, and any society that does not accept it—without regard to their experiences or cultural preferences—is immoral. This entirely normative claim will be far less persuasive if a sociologist can demonstrate that many societies, which in all other respects fulfill the criteria of a moral society, reject the particular morality or right asserted to be normatively universal.[9]

Imagine, for example, an isolated society with limited resources that respects life, reveres elders, distributes wealth fairly, and values due process. But it has a rule that when a person gets very old and infirm, he or she is placed on a drifting iceberg and, following a ceremony of respect and love, floated out to sea. All the members of that society understand their ultimate fate and accept it as part of their culture. Anthropologists prove that by employing this approach, the culture improves not only the quality of life but also its average duration. It works—for them! Yet we regard it as barbaric and immoral. It violates nearly every criterion by which we tend to judge morality and rights: Innocent people are—let's not mince words—executed. To be sure, they are not being punished for any wrongdoing, but that makes it even worse—comparable, in some respects, to eugenically inspired euthanasia of the "unfit." We cannot bring ourselves to say that what they are doing is just, but can we fairly condemn it as unjust? If we can, we must—at the very least—take into account their differing social mores in *ranking* the seriousness of the alleged injustice. We must also take into account the fact that the iceberg practice works—for them. It works not only by *their* general standards of morality but in some sense even by our own standards, despite our initial revulsion at the execution of the innocent. *They* consider it fair and humane, and although it violates some of our core values, it is difficult to articulate a persuasive argument against it based on our morals, considering the alternatives they have available.

This is what distinguishes the iceberg case from the Nazi euthanasia program, which may have "worked" when judged according to a racist ideology but not according to any widely accepted moral standards. The iceberg case shows a society that is generally moral by our standards but that employs a particular technique for allocating scarce resources that is immoral by what we believe should be universal standards, though it contributes to the overall morality of their society (as judged by our own standards). How can such a society be judged by reference to a singular, universal standard of morality or rights? Must not any judgment take into account the sociological realities of the community?

There is no one compelling standard of natural or positive law that is universally applicable. Consider the following scenario, which elaborates on the story of the old people in the isolated society and transposes it to our own society, albeit at a future time: The entire world experiences population growth that cannot be sustained by diminishing resources. Unless something can be done to curtail population size, the most vulnerable people—the very young, the very old, the very sick, the very poor, and the very weak—will begin to die.

Various proposals are put forward. They include:

- Financial inducements to limit births to one child.
- Mandatory birth limitations, enforceable by abortion and sterilization.
- Cutting off of Medicare (and comparable financial support) at age seventy-five.
- Denial of all medical services and medicines at age seventy-five, regardless of the wealth of the individual.
- Cutting off of Medicare for all people with specified chronic conditions, such as Alzheimer's disease, mental retardation, incurable cancer, or serious heart disease.
- Denial of all medical services and medicines to the above.
- Denial of all medical services and medicines to prisoners sentenced to life.
- Cutting off of Medicare to extremely sick babies.
- Denial of all medical treatment to the above.
- Mandatory life limitation to age eighty, enforceable by execution.
- Imposing capital punishment on convicted felons, or violent recidivist felons.
- Random execution of 10 percent of the population, selected by lot.

- Random killing of 25 percent of the population over sixty-five, selected by lot.
- Allowing people selected for random execution to provide a substitute, either by paying for one, getting a loved one to volunteer, or some other "fair" method.
- Letting nature take its course.

Despite enormous dedication of resources and heroic efforts, there are no "good" solutions to the problem (such as colonization of space, building ocean platforms, or cultivating new food sources). The tragic choices are limited to the above.

How would one go about choosing—or thinking about how to choose—among such terrible options? John Rawls's "original position" and "veil of ignorance" fail to provide one right answer. Rawls imagines moral beings in a netherworld, denied knowledge of their actual condition in this world, deciding on criteria for justice.[10] Decent people denied the knowledge of whether, at the operative time, they would be old or young, rich or poor, healthy or sick, black or white would still disagree about the "right" or even the self-serving option. There is no intuition of justice that necessarily leads in one direction. Ronald Dworkin's emphasis on human dignity, equality, and fairness does not provide us with the single right answer he assures us is often possible, since none of the options is completely consistent with these rights, and none is more consistent than several others. Immanuel Kant's categorical imperative would probably lead to inaction, as would most variations on traditional natural law. Traditional legal positivism would simply provide a structure for lawmaking, adjudication, and enforcement. It would provide no guidance on the substance of the positive rules.[11]

We can articulate some of the considerations that should be factored into any moral and rational decision. They might include the following: a requirement of equality and fairness, which would forbid the use of factors such as money, race, religion, or gender in determining or even influencing the decision as to who shall live and who shall die, or who shall have limits imposed on their procreation; a requirement that the state not actively take the life of innocent people; and a requirement that the state not be in the business of mandating abortion or sterilization.

If all of these considerations—which can be translated into rights—are absolute, then the only moral course of action is inaction. But doing nothing would produce the most immoral and irrational of results: the survival of the richest and strongest, the most predatory, selfish, and conniving. It should not be surprising that the application of natural law would replicate the state of nature that law was designed to overcome.

Some might respond by arguing that natural law would persuade moral people not to kill each other in order to live. Unfortunately those who followed such "natural law" would become the first victims of those who did not. Perhaps natural law would enforce its moral rules forbidding the strong from killing the weak. But how would it enforce such rules in a world where some must die so that others might live? Obviously, by killing or imprisoning those who would kill to save their own lives or those of loved ones. This might produce a just resolution whereby only those who broke the law would be killed. But even putting aside the moral objections to capital punishment, what if this deterrent were to work, in part, but executions of lawbreakers still would not sufficiently reduce the population size? The Grim Reaper would remain relentless, and those who died "natural" deaths would either be the weakest or else they would be people randomly denied food, medication, and other necessities. There are many unjust solutions to our problems—selection based on racial, religious, gender, or economic grounds. But there are no perfectly just solutions.

Some might argue that my example is invalid, since it creates a state of emergency, and no system of rights can be expected to work perfectly under such pressures. But "emergencies" are matters of degree. Throughout history, there have been many nations where people died because of inadequate resources. Even during the Holocaust, decisions akin to those outlined above had to be made. Should a crying baby be smothered to prevent Nazis from discovering the hiding place of a large group? Should a named person be turned over to the Gestapo to prevent the killing of hostages? Should food and medicine be denied the very young or very old to maximize survival of the hardiest? Tragic choices had to be made by moral people who had no morally acceptable options available to them. Some chose immorality, others chose compromise, while still others chose inaction or death. Can we judge them by a single standard of morality?

Oliver Wendell Holmes Jr. once observed that "Every society rests on the death of men"—that it is the function of governments to cause the death or prevent the birth of some to assure the lives of others.[12] Thomas Malthus made a related observation in a more empirical context. The point is that human life is too complex, too fragile, too unpredictable, too subject to perceived emergencies to be amenable to a set of simple moral rules that produce singularly right answers. Avoiding absolutely wrong answers may be the best we can do in many circumstances. And that is not trivial. During the Holocaust, few people judged their own conduct or the conduct of others by some utopian view of how to measure up to Aristotle's "most desirable way of life," but many tried hard to avoid becoming like their oppressors.

For those who believe in an absolute morality—a categorical imperative—there can be no balancing of interests or mere avoidance of absolutely wrong answers. There must be a right answer, or else we sink into moral relativism. Dostoyevsky had Ivan Karamazov put the ultimate test of relativism to his brother Alyosha: "Imagine that you are creating a fabric of human destiny with the object of making men happy in the end, giving them peace at last, but that it was essential and inevitable to torture to death only one tiny creature—that baby beating its breast with its fist, for instance—and to found that edifice on its unavenged tears, would you consent to be the architect on those conditions? Tell me, and tell the truth." Alyosha replied without hesitation: "No, I wouldn't consent."

Jeremy Bentham, too, would not have hesitated: He would argue that torturing and murdering the child was the right thing to do—just as he argued that torture was justified if it promoted the greatest happiness for the greatest number.[13] Most of us would not only hesitate, we would probably not know what we would actually do until confronted with this horrible choice of evils, as we may be if a captured terrorist refuses to divulge the target of his fellow terrorists who are planning an imminent attack.

Durkheim, while "unashamedly moralistic," believed that philosophy and morality "require . . . sociology," because "philosophical speculation about moral (including legal) matters must be grounded in comparative study of moral facts."[14] He rejected traditional natural law because he eschewed God (though this scion of a rabbinical family wrote about religion extensively and recognized its importance) and believed that human nature was constantly changing in response to nurture and culture.[15] Yet he also rejected traditional legal positivism. He viewed the law as embodying the morality of a society, in much the same way that religion does. Indeed, he saw striking parallels between the "functions" of law and religion in society: "They are both foci of duty and commitment. They impose obligations on those subject to them, who accept their authority."[16]

Durkheim was plainly wrong—both morally and empirically—when he asserted that "law is meaningless if it is detached from religion, which has given it its main distinguishing marks, and of which it is partially only a derivation."[17] If Durkheim was referring to traditional organized religions, he may have been right, descriptively, about the sources of many laws,[18] but he was demonstrably wrong about contemporary law, especially in places, like much of Europe, where many people revere law but reject religion. If he was referring to "some shared focus of belief and attachment that is necessary to every society," then he was merely stating a tautology: People will not believe in a legal system unless it reflects their shared beliefs.

Whether or not law must be based on religion (however defined) in order to be meaningful or persuasive, it is clear that Durkheim was groping toward an important insight: A successful legal system should do more than coerce compliance through the threat of punishment. It should seek to persuade its constituents to obey the law because that is the right and just thing to do. For this mechanism of moral internalization to work, the law must be perceived to be just, and for it to be so perceived it must—according to Durkheim—actually *be* just, as evaluated against the needs of the particular society.

Durkheim sought to break down the high walls of separation between philosophy and empiricism, between morality and pragmatism, between religion and law, between what ought to be and what is. He realized, of course, that the primary role of sociology—the discipline he helped create—was to describe existing societies, while the primary role of the normative disciplines, especially moral philosophy, was to prescribe what is right and wrong.* But he asked, "By what privilege is the philosopher to be permitted to speculate about society, without entering into commerce with the detail of social facts?" And in a blistering attack on the ivory tower philosopher,

---

*Advocates of natural law and advocates of positive law are really asking two different questions. Although both appear to be addressing themselves to the sources of law, they use *sources* in different ways. The natural-law advocate, by seeking sources outside of positive law, is really asking about how we *evaluate* existing law. The legal positivist describes existing law and seeks sources in the lawmaking process.

he demanded that "moral issues be posed and addressed in the light of systematic study of experience since we are in no way justified in seeing in the personal aspirations that the thinker feels . . . an adequate expression of moral reality."[19]

In my estimation, this gives a bit too much weight to the empirical component of morality and too little to its speculative element. Moral philosophers should be encouraged to speculate freely about the *oughts* of life without being limited by the *is* of any given society, but these speculations must be tested against the realities of human experience. Durkheim's concept of "moral reality" seeks to bridge the gap between the normative (moral) and the empirical (reality), but it poses the danger of accepting what is without asking what might be. (This mirrors the Alexander Pope fallacy "whatever is, is right," and the Shavian reply, "I dream things that never were; and I say, 'Why not?'") In this regard, it is reminiscent of those natural-law and morality advocates who believe that "all nature is good." While Durkheim was never so naïve as to believe that all society is good, he gave too much weight to the moral "common sense" of existing society and too little to the abstract, a priori speculations of ivory tower philosophers such as Kant, Hegel, or Bentham[20] (just as some ivory tower philosophers gave too little weight to sociological realities).

While Durkheim is surely correct that "experience alone can decide if [particular abstract moral philosophies] are suitable" to a time and place,[21] I insist that "suitability" is not the only criterion for evaluating the justice of a society's "moral reality." An amoral sociologist would conclude that the moral reality of Nazi Germany was ideally "suited" to its social structure and ideology. That would not make it right or just. Durkheim's response would be that such a society would eventually be destroyed, by either internal or external force.[22] Well, maybe! Just because that happened to the Nazis is no guarantee of its inevitability. (Had just a few historical contingencies been altered—had the Nazis developed an atomic bomb before we did, or had the Hitler–Stalin pact remained intact—the outcome of World War II might have been different.) There must be an external standard for evaluating a society's morality beyond "suitability."*

The problem is that no such external standard actually exists in nature or in the word of God. The only way it can emerge is if it is constructed on the basis of the broader experiences of the entire world over time, rather than the limited experiences of one particular society at a single point in its history. The need for basic universal standards for defining and even enforcing the most fundamental human rights is clear from the experiences of the world in the twentieth century alone. Constructing mechanisms for defining and enforcing these standards, with due concern for the variations made necessary by different cultural and experiential factors, is the great human challenge we face. We cannot abdicate it to God or nature. It is our job, our responsibility, and our challenge to construct such mechanisms. In meeting this challenge, we must look to experience, to nature, and to the a priori speculations of philosophers, moralists, and other thinkers. The difficult question is how these elements are to coalesce in the interest of a morality that is both just and workable. Durkheim's contribution to this never-ending

---

*John Stuart Mill disagreed with his mentor Bentham on precisely this. Presciently, he postulated an evil society that maximized the happiness of most of its citizens (e.g., Aryans) at the expense of a small oppressed minority (e.g., Jews). Such a society might satisfy Bentham's maximization of happiness principle, but it would not satisfy Mill's requirement of individual rights. Mill sought to reconcile his insistence on individual rights with utilitarianism by postulating "utilities which are vastly more important, and therefore, more absolute and imperative" than the mere promotion of human pleasure (quoted in Hart, *Essays*, pp. 188–190). Mill, the moral utilitarian, derived this hierarchy of utilities—what he called primary moralities—from some standard external both to law and to the philosophy of utilitarianism. He is vague about the source of this standard, beyond the somewhat circular contention that it is necessary for human happiness.

quest for the just society is both invaluable and incomplete, especially as it relates to individual rights.

Durkheim tried "implicitly to solve the problems which positivist jurists have long associated with attempts to make law and morality analytically inseparable"[23] by insisting that law itself—positive law—must have a moral component. He saw the law as something "worth giving loyalty to," because it is the embodiment of society's morality. But he failed to solve the problem of how to evaluate, and whether to comply with, unjust laws that suit an unjust society, or whether basic rights "exist" in a society that has decided that such rights do not suit it.*

Durkheim's concept of rights and their sources changed over time. His early writings presented rights as "bestowed by the state on the individual," in order to serve a societal function. They do not attach at birth, do not inhere in the individual, and "are not inscribed in the nature of things." His later works referred to rights and liberties being conferred on man by the "sacredness with which he is invested." This suggests a divine source, but it seems likely that Durkheim was using the term in its broad, metaphorical sense. Durkheim eventually came to believe that certain basic rights—particularly "freedom of thought"—were moral entitlements as well as societal necessities.[24] But their source or sources, and hence whether he considered them inalienable or merely functional, were never persuasively articulated beyond his view that morality is—in

---

*Durkheim saw no sharp line between philosophical and sociological views of morality, since he regarded morality as a function of the particular society rather than as universal or timeless. "As such it is relative, yet not a matter of preference" (Cotterrell, *Émile Durkheim*, p. 203). H. L. A. Hart took Durkheim's challenge a step further by arguing that "there is, in the very notion of law consisting of general rules, something which prevents us from treating it as if morally it is utterly neutral, without any necessary contact with moral principles" (Hart, *Essays*, p. 81). Yet he acknowledges that a legal system could be moral in its application by being equally applicable to all, while being immoral in its substance.

a general sense—the source of law and religion. As religion evolves into law, it recognizes the capacity of individuals to view rules critically and to challenge them[25] on the basis of experience.[26] Debate and communication then become more important in the formulation of morality and rights, leading to the democratic processes of governance that Durkheim believed were essential to the modern state whose primary function is "to liberate individual personalities" and "to provide a realm of basic individual freedoms."[27]

Eventually Durkheim became a zealous advocate of rights, premised on the need for "individualism," which provided "the moral spine" of modern law. But while the need for these freedoms or rights became clear in Durkheim's later writings, their source remained obscure, as it does today in the writings of many of our most brilliant secular philosophers and thinkers. Perhaps as Durkheim himself experienced and observed more human injustice, he came to appreciate the need for rights as a necessary mechanism to slow down the human penchant for injustice—for inflicting wrongs. Had he lived later in the twentieth century, Durkheim would have seen even more wrongs—and he would have appreciated rights even more. It is no coincidence that we experienced a burgeoning of human rights in the aftermath of the Second World War.

A theory of rights that is based on experiences with wrongs breaks down the high wall between philosophy and sociology, between the ought and the is, between the normative and the empirical. It seeks to find a proper balance among human experience, human nature, and abstract notions of right and wrong. It is a never-ending quest.

CHAPTER 12

Can Rights Produce Wrongs?

MOST, THOUGH NOT all, jurisprudential theorists construct elaborate frameworks of principle and theories of rights that just happen to lead them to the promised land of policies they favor on political, religious, or personal grounds. I am not suggesting that it is always deliberate or conscious. Broad principles and specific policies are related, of course, and it should not be surprising that "liberal" or "conservative" principles—to use imprecise but familiar terms—will often lead to liberal or conservative policies.[1] It is the rare scholar whose rigorous commitment to intellectual honesty, principle, and consistency leads him to construct a theory of rights that produces results inconsistent with his personal, political, and economic views. John Ely was among that rare breed. His theory of rights (which was part of his more general theory of judicial review in a democracy) often led him to results that clashed with his personal preferences. For example, he opposed *Roe v. Wade,* but he supported a woman's right to choose.

The arguments made by Southern intellectual and religious leaders in defense of slavery before and during the Civil War provide a perfect example of the human capacity to construct after-the-fact arguments in support of almost any morally disputed practice. Brilliant and honest intellectuals invoked natural law, biblical law, the rules of political economy, and virtually every other method of reasoning known to humans. They defended slavery as a "right"—a right not only of the slave owner but also of the slave!

John C. Calhoun invoked natural law to "prove" the inferiority of blacks, as Jefferson had cited nature several decades earlier.[2] And several pre–Civil War state constitutions declared the "right" to own slaves as "before and higher than any constitutional sanction."[3]

Invoking divine law, advocates of slavery pointed to the biblical description of the patriarch Abraham's slave-owning family. In the words of historian Eugene Genovese, "Abraham was, in their oft-expressed view, simultaneously a slaveholder and God's favorite patriarch of a household that included many slaves."[4] Even Calhoun, regarded by many as a moderate, cited "Hebrew theocracy" as the greatest government man had ever experienced and "held up the extended household under the firm authority of its male as the model for its organization."[5] This concept of "Christian slavery" was designed, according to these arguments, to save the souls of the black slave. Hence, the right to be a slave in order to be saved.[6]

Slavery, it was claimed, was the "natural and proper condition of all labor" and the foundation of all freedom. But what of the civil and political rights of the slave? "Led by Calhoun, the Southern theorist overwhelmingly accepted natural law but vehemently rejected the attempts to deduce natural rights from it," especially civil and political rights. Some did argue for natural rights but limited them to certain statuses: "the rights of the father are natural, but they belong only to the father." The same was true of the right of property; it belonged "only to those who had property"—namely, the slave owner. No rights belonged to the property itself, namely, the slave. Even for those who regarded slaves as more than property, the only right the slave had was the right to be treated decently, the way slaves were supposed to be treated in the Bible. "Slaveholders are responsible . . . for the humane treatment of their fellow human beings whom God has placed in their hands."[7]

Some Southern religious writers even made evolutionary claims. One such writer jumped from Genesis to Darwin with hardly a pause, asserting that while God created white people "after the image of the Creator,"[8] there was a continuum of intelligence between "the ape tribes" and lower humans. He postulated a future time when apes would have progressed to the point where they "should learn to speak," and he asked, rhetorically, whether they should then "be placed on an equality with whites, as they indicate somewhat of a human form and intelligence so as relates to the performance of labor!" His answer—a resounding no—was supposed to resolve the issue of equality between the white race, which was created in the image of God, and the black race, which was created "for subordinate works."[9] (For some, this time in the future has arrived. There are now proponents of human rights for great apes. In 1999, New Zealand became the first nation to adopt a law guaranteeing certain rights to great apes. Several years earlier, scientist Carl Sagan had posed the following question: "If chimpanzees have consciousness, if they are capable of abstractions, do they not have what until now has been described as 'human rights'?"[10])

Southern intellectuals also invoked economic and political arguments in support of slavery. They pointed to the dreadful situation of "free laborers" in the North and throughout Europe, and the exploitative nature of industrial capitalism. The slave owner felt a moral obligation toward the slave and had an economic stake in his continued welfare, since the slave was valuable property. The capitalist treated his worker as disposable and replaceable. Southern intellectuals rejected socialism and its variants as an alternative to capitalist exploitation, since it could not be brought about without the instabilities seen throughout Europe in the mid-nineteenth century. For Southern intellectuals, the only real alternatives were pure exploitative capitalism or pure paternalistic slavery. The choice for them was clear.

Finally, there was the political argument, which rejected the natural-law claims made by Northern abolitionists against secession and slavery. Pointing to the contractual nature of our constitutional system—a "political compromise between two sectionally based social systems"[11]—the Southerners argued that the North had no right to impose its system on the South. Invoking the rhetoric of the founding fathers, they cited the Declaration of Independence as the source of their right to secede and maintain their slave-based social system. As far as the right of every slave to be a free laborer, they mocked this as the right to be "free to beg, steal and starve."

In reading these arguments, which sound so lame and baldly immoral to the contemporary ear, one is repeatedly struck by their sincerity. These people actually believed what they were saying. They believed that slavery was right, and they believed in the arguments they were making in justification of this institution.

This process of justification illustrates the complex relationship between a priori and experiential reasoning. Some of the arguments offered in favor of slavery derive directly from external sources—the Bible, natural law, or some logical construct. Others are based on observations and experiences. Each type of argument is invoked in support of the other, and it is never clear which comes first. It is as if a certain number of "argument cards" were distributed to each player in this game of advocacy. Some cards trump others. Some types of cards lead the player down one path or another. A good player knows how to think ahead several moves and anticipate the countermoves of his or her opponent. Experienced advocates have heard it all—every conceivable argument for every conceivable practice, made with sincerity, passion, consistency, authority, and other tools of advocacy. (As the old saw goes: Sincerity is the essence of acting; if you can fake that, you can fake anything.) They cannot avoid a certain degree of cynicism regarding the human capacity to persuade oneself and others about the virtues of a particular point of view at a particular point in time.[12] It is no wonder then that Wendell Phillips, an abolitionist who had once invoked natural rights against slavery, eventually came to realize that "because 'nature' no longer spoke with a single voice, only the judge's conscience ultimately determined the source of rights."[13] But it is not that nature "no longer" spoke with a single voice that makes the quest for natural rights futile; it is that nature alone cannot speak about rights at all. Nor can "the judge's conscience" be the source of rights, since every judge has a different conscience. In the *Dred Scott* decision of 1857,[14] Justice Roger Tawney's conscience concluded that slaves are property without rights, while a century later Justice Earl Warren's conscience concluded that descendants of former slaves have the right to nonsegregated education alongside the descendants of former slave owners.[15]

In previous chapters we have seen how "rights" have led to other wrongs as well. Rights do not guarantee the "right" result. Like any other construct, they can be manipulated to serve any agenda. Yet if rights are designed to eliminate or slow down the recurrence of the most grievous historical wrongs, there is less likelihood that they will be misused.

For true advocates of liberty's agenda, the continuing struggle is to represent a genuine and deep-seated commitment to civil liberties and human rights without regard for the political agendas of the day. For such long-view civil libertarians, a rights-based system is essential regardless of who or what it happens to benefit at any particular moment in history. Thus, freedom of speech is as desirable in the newly liberated nations of the former Soviet Union, where it may immediately benefit racists and anti-Semites, as it is in China, where the main beneficiaries would be democratic dissidents. It is the long-term benefits of a rights-based system that help to avoid repetition of the wrongs of the past.

But for many, the demand for civil rights and liberties is merely a temporary tactic designed to support immediate political goals. For such people, rights are merely temporary preferences, to be abandoned once they no longer serve some political or other interest. For example, the hierarchy of the Polish Catholic Church was in the vanguard of rights and liberty when Soviet Communism was in control of Poland. The church advocated freedom of speech, freedom of conscience, educational choice, and other fundamental freedoms as a tactic to undercut the totalitarianism of communist rule. But when communism crumbled and the church itself once again became a dominant political force in Poland, the agenda of liberty was generally forsaken, and the agenda of authority—its own authority—was advocated by many in the church hierarchy. Civil rights and liberties had been little more than a convenient tactic in the overall strategy of church domination. A similar phenomenon has been at work in Israel, where the fervently religious minority has employed democracy as a tactic for enhancing its immediate power, while eschewing democracy when it conflicts with its long-term theocratic goals.

This tactical use and abuse of civil liberties to serve other agendas has been a recurring theme in modern history. Even Thomas Jefferson was guilty of the double standard. Before he held high office, he famously quipped, "Were it left to me to decide whether we should have a government without newspapers, or newspapers without a government, I should not hesitate a moment to prefer the latter." But after twenty years of public service, his views changed. In 1807 he said of his formerly beloved newspapers: "the man who never looks into a newspaper is better informed than he who reads them, insomuch as he who knows nothing is nearer the truth than he whose mind is filled with falsehoods and error." Likewise with Václav Havel, whose Velvet Revolution in Czechoslovakia demanded a free press, but who, after serving as president, wondered out loud whether the press was "too free" in criticizing him. Some might argue—in defense of the church, Jefferson, Havel, and others—that their own experiences tempered their perspective on rights. This is undeniably true. But because the changes were so completely in line with their interests, it is difficult to avoid the charge of the self-serving double standard.

The historical and experiential change that is most relevant to constructing rights occurs over a more sustained period and relates to a broader segment of society than to the individual (or elites) who have ascended to power. Beware of those whose advocacy of individual rights changes quickly when these same rights begin to curtail their own recently acquired power. Throughout history we have also seen the courageous struggle for liberty's agenda, often led by lonely advocates with no immediate personal or partisan stake in liberty's triumph, but with an abiding commitment to liberty for the sake of human dignity, and for the sake of preventing recurrence of past wrongs.

Rights can indeed produce wrongs, because it is in the nature of rights that they serve as a check on the certainty of popular opinions. If rights are human inventions based on our experience with wrongs, then it is certainly possible for human beings to misunderstand the lessons of experience or to fail to recognize wrongs. It is also possible to misuse rights—to hijack them for narrow, temporary, partisan gain. Rights do not guarantee the right outcome. A world with rights is a world with risks, but experience teaches that a world without rights is a world with even greater risks.

CHAPTER 13

Is the Debate over External Sources of Rights a Liberal-Conservative Issue?

T HOSE WHO ADVOCATE natural law, as distinguished from more consequentialist and positivist approaches, do not divide along traditional liberal-conservative or progressive-reactionary lines. Ronald Dworkin, among the most influential contemporary proponents of an independent source of rights beyond existing law and mere utility, happens to be a liberal-progressive who identifies with the left in both politics and constitutional law. Richard Posner, among the most influential proponents of a positivist and consequentialist approach to rights, is far more conservative and identifies with the right.* Many advocates of natural law (especially divine natural law) tend to be on the right, while many consequentialists see themselves as closer to the left. But Dworkin's natural-law (or, more precisely, nonpositivist and nonconsequentialist) approach generally leads him to (some might say follows from) his progressive views, and Posner's more consequen-

---

*It is interesting to note that Dworkin and Posner have each constructed theories that play to their own individual strengths. Dworkin has few peers in his ability to formulate general theories, draw apt distinctions, and shift levels of abstraction so as to achieve consistency. Posner has few peers in his ability to use economic analysis to justify his personal and political views. Both approaches have in common their inaccessibility to the general public and their dependence on the esoteric arguments of intellectual elites.

tialist approach nearly always leads him to (or follows from) his more conservative views.

Neither natural law nor legal positivism has any necessary correlation—in theory or in practice—to either radical or reactionary programs. Each has been employed in the service of both revolution and preservation of the status quo. Natural law has served as justification for the American Revolution, for slave rebellions, for acts of civil disobedience, and for reformist changes in the law. By invoking a higher authority, radical advocates of natural law have sought to justify the violation of unjust positive law or the overthrow of unjust systems of law. Reactionary advocates of natural law have also invoked higher authority as a justification for religious oppression, denial of positive-law rights (reproductive freedom, assisted suicide, fetal cell transplantation), and the preservation of the status quo (slavery, criminalization of homosexuality).

Legal positivists, too, have been revolutionaries, disobedients, and reformers. For them the law is the law, but often "the law is a ass—a idiot" (to use the phrase of Charles Dickens's character, Mr. Bumble, in *Oliver Twist*) that must be changed, and positive law can be unmade by human beings as easily as it was made by them. Legal positivism was born of reformist parents such as Jeremy Bentham, John Austin, and John Stuart Mill. It then gave birth to some of the most oppressive systems of legal, political, and military tyranny. "Law is law," said the Nazis, and no one had the right to invoke any higher authority as a justification for disobeying it.

The idea that there are no external sources for law or morality and that human beings create these sources according to their own values has long been associated with the amoral philosophy of Friedrich Nietzsche, whose values were thoroughly obnoxious. But there is no necessary correlation between the denial of an objective morality and the human construction of any particular subjective morality. The fact that Nietzsche's personal morality was elitist, racist, sexist, and undemocratic simply illustrates the risks of leaving moral choice to individuals. Some will choose badly, while others will create elevated and compassionate moralities that are as good as or better than anything found in natural law or so-called objective morality. I need mention only Mill's and Robert Nozick's as examples of humanly constructed moral systems that are as different from Nietzsche's proto-Nazism as any philosophies can be.

Even if it were true—which it surely is not—that untethering morality from religion or other allegedly external sources would inevitably lead to Nietzsche or "cannibalism" (as the Grand Inquisitor suggests), that would only be an argument in favor of the *desirability of* and *need for* an objective morality derived from an external source. It would not be an argument in favor of its *actual existence.* If no such morality, in fact, exists, we have only a handful of basic alternatives to purely subjective, individualistic morality:

1. We can *pretend* it exists and act as if it did. We may call this the moral-fiction approach.
2. We can try to *derive* an objective morality from sources that do exist, such as human nature. We may call this the derivative approach.
3. We can try to *construct* a system of morality that is so logically compelling that we make a plausible claim of objectivity for it. We may call this the objective-constructive approach.
4. We can look to the *experiences* of human beings over time—especially negative experiences—and draw lessons from them that serve as a basis for an ever-changing, humanly created system of morality, law, and rights, and advocate certain rights based on these experiences. We may call this the experiential-advocacy approach.

There is nothing inherently liberal or conservative about any of these approaches. Each is an attempt to *describe* sources of law and rights, and descriptions do not necessarily carry normative implications and certainly do not mandate particular moral conclusions. Each of these approaches can produce good or evil, progress or regress, liberalism or conservatism.

To the extent that some approaches to natural law suggest that its content is universal and eternal, it is—at least in theory—more difficult to change than positive law, which is—also in theory—easily amendable. But natural law has, of course, changed dramatically over the years, and its purported content varies from place to place as well as from time to time. Positive law has sometimes been more enduring. The United States Constitution, which is positive law, has endured with few changes for more than two centuries, whereas its "natural-law" underpinnings have changed in numerous respects over the same period. The durability of positive law is, of course, a double-edged sword, since bad positive laws may also endure, especially when they deprive citizens of the right to dissent and to seek change in the law.

At an even more fundamental level, the debate between those who seek moral constraints outside of the positive law and those who eschew external constraints is a disagreement about trusting human beings with freedom. The most powerful case against such trust was made by Dostoyevsky's Grand Inquisitor, who believed that science (or economics) without the authoritative constraints of religion would inevitably lead to the internal anxiety of untrammeled freedom and the external catastrophe of cannibalism (and, we might now add, terrorism and nuclear destruction). The case for trust is made by Bentham, Mill, Posner, and others who believe that external moral constraints are nonsense and that human beings must be free, as Oliver Wendell Holmes Jr. liked to say, to make bad choices: "If my fellow citizens want to go to hell, I will help them."[1]

Among the most compelling proofs that rights grow out of the experiences of humankind and not some abstract, external source is the very history of the epistemology of rights. The nature of the debate over the source of rights has itself been a function of the experiences of the time. Bentham rejected natural law because he had witnessed its abuses. Utilitarianism and legal positivism had their intellectual heydays during a period of great reform. They fell into disrepute following the Nazi era. Now that we have experienced the abuses of both natural law and positivist utilitarianism, we crave other theories that provide the benefits of each without their difficulties. We search for a utilitarianism that does not sacrifice individuals or small groups to the happiness of the many—that treats individuals as deserving of respect and consideration regardless of the consequences to the many. We seek to discover, create, or construct a natural law that is not dependent on God's word, nature's message, or some other metaphysical source. We know that we need a source of rights beyond the law, the utilitarian calculus, the word of God, or the demands of nature! But we cannot "find" it, for the simple reason that it does not exist outside of human experience.

Law and morality are the constructs of human beings struggling to elevate themselves from the state of nature—to reinforce the human capacity for good and to discourage the capacity for evil. All we can do is articulate and advocate those rights that experience teaches us are essential to avoid the catastrophes of the past,* recognizing that if we fail to understand the lessons of history, we may be doomed to repeat its horrors. Once a consensus emerges that we should try to avoid the recurrence of certain wrongs, we can begin

---

*H. L. A. Hart talks about "the rough seas which the philosophy of political morality is presently crossing between the old faith in utilitarianism and the new faith in rights." *Essays in Jurisprudence and Philosophy* (New York: Oxford University Press, 1983), p. 221. He is more cautiously optimistic than I am that hard work by moral philosophers will eventually lead us to the holy grail of a perfect theory of rights with a legitimate source of authority.

to build a system of rights. Central to this building process is continuous advocacy of rights that experience shows can help prevent
the recurrence of these wrongs.

The experiential approach to rights is located, in one sense,
somewhere between the Dworkin–Posner poles, but in another
sense it lies outside the debate. It serves as a practical guide to action in the absence of a definitive resolution of the age-old debate
between advocates of natural and of positive law. While philosophers continue to refine the esoteric issues of "externality" and
"constructivity," practitioners of rights—those who *do* rights, who
advocate and enforce them—cannot remain on hold. An experientially based, bottom-up approach to rights allows the practitioner
to look to history as a guide to which rights could have prevented
or slowed down the injustices of the past and might therefore serve
as a check on the injustices of the future. This is, in fact, an apt account of how many people—even including many philosophers—
actually arrive at their approach to rights.

One may thus reject the *program* offered by the Grand Inquisitor—surrender to authority, miracle, and mystery—while agreeing
in large part with his *description* of human nature. Advocates of
rights must struggle against the inherent need of most people for
external authority by trying to persuade them not to submit to the
seductive Grand Inquisitors of every generation—those who would
take away their anxiety-producing freedom of choice and offer them
in its place the comfort of believing that others (God, the church,
the king, the president, the judge, the economist, or the philosopher) have the responsibility of choosing for them.

Professor Albert Alschuler bemoans the fact—as he sees it—that
"the central lyric of twentieth-century American jurisprudence [has
been] 'Ain't no wrong, ain't no right.'"[2] To the extent that this lyric
suggests there are no absolute rules of morality dictated by God, na-

ture, or reason alone, I agree. But wrong and right (especially wrong) can and must be induced from experience. Our moral obligation is clear: We must *build* a system of right and wrong precisely because these important moral principles do not exist outside of human experience. We must articulate and advocate rights that will help to prevent recurrence of the terrible wrongs of the past.[3] We must invent our own morality—and induce our own rights from experience—because there is nobody else to do it for us.

III *Applying the Experiential Theory of Rights to Specific Controversies*

CHAPTER 14

Can Experiential Rights Check the Abuses of Majority Rule?

ANY THEORY OF rights must demonstrate its utility by addressing real problems. In the remaining chapters, I apply the experiential theory of rights to some enduring issues—such as the "right to life," freedom of speech, separation of church and state, and terrorism. But first I take a more general look at rights as an important part of our system of checks and balances.

How Rights Function in a Democracy

If rights are trumps on majority preferences, then they must be justified by reference either to democratic principles or to other principles that transcend democracy. Positive-law rights that were originally entrenched by representative institutions—such as constitutional conventions, legislatures, or referenda—are an outgrowth of the democratic process. The only question is whether democratic decisions of the past should be binding on today's majorities. So long as they can be changed by an amending process—even a super-majoritarian process—the elements of democracy are still present.* When rights purport to come from external sources, such as God or nature, they

---

*A super-majoritarian process is one that requires more than a simple majority. For example, it requires more than a majority to amend the Constitution or to remove a president from office.

can claim no democratic source (unless the majority agrees to be bound by such external sources).

The irony—repeated throughout history—is that it is generally citizens themselves who want rights curtailed in the name of safety, security, or convenience. Sometimes the reasons are even less compelling: bigotry, xenophobia, and intolerance. The greatest crises for a constitutional democracy occur when the majority demands that minority rights be abridged in the name of strongly held preferences or claims of necessity. The conflict between the power of the many and the rights of the few raises the most profound questions about our theory of government.

How does a democracy justify a Bill of Rights that allows a minority to overrule the majority? At a simple level, the answer is clear: The Bill of Rights is democratically enacted (though by a public with limited franchise) and can be democratically repealed (though by a complex super-majoritarian process). But if these rights were ever to be repealed by law, many would still argue that these rights (and others) are unalienable because their source—God or nature—transcends democracy. Others would argue in response that in a democracy, only the law can be a source of rights. Advocates of experiential rights would point to the wrongs that led to the acceptance of these rights and argue that these wrongs (and others) are likely to recur if rights are abrogated.

Throughout our history of constitutional democracy, efforts have been periodically made to justify minority restraints on majority action. Although no single rationale has gained universal acceptance, the general consensus has been that the constitutional experiment— really a series of ever-changing experiments—has worked. Experience has shown that the greatest threats to our liberty have come from transient majorities intolerant of the rights of minorities: the Alien and Sedition Acts, white ownership of black slaves, Know-Nothing nativism and persecution of immigrants, segregation and racism, anti-Japanese hysteria culminating in the detention of more than 100,000 Americans, the pernicious thought control of McCarthyism, and the ethnic profiling and detention of Arabs and Muslims following the attacks of September 11, 2001. Our Bill of Rights has provided less-than-perfect protection against these excesses, but it has contributed to the prevention of popular tyranny. The first ten amendments have also occasionally imposed some severe—and in retrospect perhaps unnecessary—checks on popular majoritarian action. For example, during the early New Deal, some important legislation designed to counter the Depression was declared to be in violation of due process. Today many Americans believe the Warren Court went too far in protecting the rights of persons accused of crime. Whether or not one agrees with these assessments, it seems clear that, in general, a workable balance has been struck between the power of the majority and the rights of minorities.

This balance is part of our dynamic system of governing, which eschews too much concentration of power. American sovereignty, unlike that of most other Western democracies, does not reside in one branch of government or even in the majority of the people. Our sovereignty is a process, reflected in governmental concepts such as checks and balances, separation of powers, and judicial review. More broadly it is reflected in freedom of the press, separation of church from state, academic freedom, the free-market economy, antitrust laws, and other structural and judicial mechanisms that make concentration of power difficult. It is also reflected in our immigration laws, which—with some striking exceptions during the 1920s and 1930s—have produced the most diverse nation in history.

Beyond these abstract concepts is a commonsense distrust of untrammeled authority, born of the varied histories and experiences that comprise the American character. We are different from most other nations in that most of our forebears chose to leave other places for a better—and freer—life.[1] We are a nation of minorities, dissidents, émigrés, risk takers, skeptics, heretics, experimenters, nay-sayers—distrustful and ornery mavericks. We are a tyrant's nightmare and an anarchist's dream. Our slogans—anachronistic as they may seem—tell us something profound about our individualism: Don't tread on me; Give me liberty or give me death; Show me; Question authority.[2]

Yesterday's quaint slogans have become today's rude bumper stickers, T-shirt logos, and graffiti. Whatever the medium, the American message has been similar for more than two centuries: We need breathing room; We will not submit to regimentation; We demand our rights.

Against this historical landscape, the Bill of Rights can best be viewed as an insurance policy against tyranny. As with all insurance policies, paying the premiums is no fun. We get nothing material in return—at least, not right away. We pay a heavy premium every time a guilty criminal is freed in the name of the Fourth Amendment, every time a pornographer or a racist is permitted to disseminate filth or poison because of the First Amendment, every time a young girl is allowed to make the "wrong" decision regarding abortion on the grounds of choice, and every time an indigent yeshiva or Catholic school student is denied a subsidized religious education because it would violate the constitutional prohibition against the government's establishing religion.

But as with an insurance policy, we pay these premiums in exchange for protection against disasters that are specifically unpredictable and generally inevitable. No insurance policy can prevent death or disability, but it can ease their ravages. Sometimes a good insurance policy even reduces risks by requiring those in control to take precautions.

The Bill of Rights, and rights in general, cannot by themselves prevent oppression. But rights impose barriers to tyranny, especially the tyranny of transient majorities seeking to entrench their power and extend it over time. A rights-based system also sends an important message to those who would seek power through dubious means: "We Americans take our rights seriously, and you ignore that message at considerable political risk." The downfalls of Richard Nixon and Joseph McCarthy are eloquent testimony to the American allergy to trashing constitutional safeguards.[3]

Over the past two hundred years, we have paid many constitutional premiums and accumulated much equity in our collective insurance policy. Fortunately, ours is not merely a term policy. It is a whole-life investment in our future as a free country.

Where Does the Burden of Proof Lie?

There are those today who would turn our Constitution into a narrow sectarian tool for the advancement of particular philosophies, doctrines, and even religions. The evangelist Pat Robertson has called the Constitution a Christian document and has promised to rescue it from "non-Christian" judges who have been misconstruing it in a secular manner. Some politicians view the Bill of Rights as an encumbrance to their political programs. They seek to have it interpreted narrowly to implement its "original intent"—an intent they claim to know. But if there was any original intent of the framers, it was general and broad: to create an enduring charter of liberty capable of responding to changing conditions.[4]

We are a very different nation today than we were in 1787. From an agrarian society composed almost exclusively of English Protestants, we have evolved into the most heterogeneous, multiethnic, multilingual, multiracial, multireligious society in the history of the world. Technologically, economically, militarily, culturally, and in so many other ways, we live in a society that the framers could not have imagined or planned for. But they gave us a document for the ages, capable of adapting to the changing experiences of the society it governs. New wrongs, unimagined by our founding fathers, must generate new rights capable of preventing the recurrence of these wrongs.

The effect of entrenching rights in a democracy is to eliminate certain issues from the control of the current majority. Put another way, it places certain entrenched rights outside the sphere of pure democracy. But if rights are not divine, natural, or eternal, and are a product of the experiences and history of a people, then there is some burden to justify their antidemocratic character. I do not see rights, properly limited, as antithetical to democracy properly defined. Rather they are the most important elements of the system of checks and balances within a democracy.[5]

Rights should not prevent all change, especially if they themselves are subject to constant reevaluation based on the changing experiences of the people. Rights do slow down certain kinds of change, under certain circumstances. Spiro Agnew, criticizing liberals who insisted on exercising their rights, once characterized individual rights as a "headwind blowing in the face of the ship of state." It is an apt metaphor, though Agnew did not mean it in its positive sense. Rights in a democracy serve to put pressure on government to change course, to move cautiously, to protect important and enduring values from precipitous abrogation—to learn the lessons of the past and avoid the wrongs of earlier generations. Judge Learned Hand once observed that when liberty dies in the hearts of men and women, "no court can save it; . . . no court can even do much to help it."[6] He was right about the first part of his observation: Courts alone cannot save liberty. But he was wrong about the second part: Courts can, by properly enforcing rights, slow down the process of tyranny—at least sometimes, as they did during the McCarthy period.[7]

Rights work, in part, by taking certain powers away from temporary majorities and vesting the capability to constrain these powers in those who lack traditional political influence or who are otherwise subject to discrimination or marginalization. Some rights actually kers that his claim should be treated as a right.* As history and experience change, the persuasiveness of a particular claim may also change. But history and experience change more gradually than shifting majoritarian preferences. In this respect, rights that are not clearly entrenched are always subject to reevaluation over time.

The judiciary, under this approach, is generally limited to slowing down change rather than preventing it. The New Deal is a perfect example of this process at work. During President Roosevelt's first term, the Supreme Court repeatedly ruled that progressive social legislation made necessary by the Depression violated the Constitution's broad requirement of due process. But changing history and experience eventually made it abundantly clear that the high court's conception of property rights (based on substantive due process) was anachronistic and unsuited to the changing economic realities of American life. It required the appointment of new justices—New Deal Democrats such as Professors Felix Frankfurter and William O. Douglas, as well as Senator Hugo Black—to turn the court around. The appointment process is thus part of the mechanism for change, just as the legal doctrine of *stare decisis* (deference to precedent) is part of the mechanism for slowing down change.

I could cite many other examples to demonstrate the wisdom of the observation that the life of the law has been experience rather than logic—or God, or nature, or any other universal and immutable truth or external source.

Do We Have Too Many Rights?

Experience has shown that new rights constantly emerge from new wrongs or a recognition of the wrongness of old practices. Consider,

---

*The rights claimant can also point to the argument that our government, particularly our federal government, is one of limited powers and that the "powers not delegated to the United States by the Constitution . . . are reserved to the States . . . or to the people." Tenth Amendment. See also Ninth Amendment.

open up the channels of democracy: free speech, equali
and protection against the establishment of religion.[8] C
of rights allow democracy to operate more fairly. I
Churchill was right when he said that a democracy should
by the manner in which it treats its most despised member:
rights of accused criminals, aliens, the mentally ill, and ot
ginalized people are an important part of the democratic pr

In a democratic system, the unelected judiciary must ha
limited power to overrule current majority preferences. Wl
Constitution is clear about a particular right trumping a p
ence—as with the right against compelled self-incrimination
riding our preference for swift conviction of the guilty—then
tivism prevails, and we do not worry about the source or legitir
of the right. The plain language of the Constitution governs.
only way to change a clearly expressed constitutional right is by
cumbersome and rarely used process of formal amendment.[9] Wh
the claimed right is not explicitly in the Constitution—as with th
rights of parents to forbid grandparents from visiting a child—thei
process should prevail, accompanied by inevitable conflict over the
source and legitimacy of the claimed right and counterright. In these
latter instances, which are far more common than the former, those
who claim that a right should trump a majoritarian preference have
the burden of establishing why their own preference deserves to be
treated as a right. It will not do, in a nontheological democracy, to
claim that God's will or nature's mandate trumps the majority.

The burden rests on them because in the absence of a compelling
claim of right, democracy demands that majoritarian preferences
prevail over minority preferences. Majority rule should be the default position in a democracy. In seeking to satisfy the burden of
demonstrating why a claimed right not explicit in the Constitution
should trump majority preferences, the rights claimant can properly
point to history and experience in an effort to persuade decision-

for example, the relatively new concept of environmental rights, which is obviously a response to the relatively new assaults on the environment growing out of modern industrialism. Though environmentalist concerns trace their origins to the biblical prohibition against destroying the fruit-bearing trees of a conquered people, the more recent experiences of industrialized nations have turned this concern into a nascent "right." I recall visiting a preindustrial country with high unemployment and low productivity and being told, "What this country needs is a little more pollution!" The history and experiences of that nation did not yet reflect a need for environmental protection and rights.

But less developed nations may have a heightened experiential need for positive economic rights—such as the right to a job, or to decent health care. The Nobel Prize–winning economist Amartya Sen has convincingly shown that there exists an inexorable relationship between political and economic rights. He points to the startling fact that no functioning democracy with political rights has ever experienced a famine, and argues that the most basic rights should include a mix of traditional negative political rights (e.g., the government may not restrict freedom of speech, religion, and so on) and positive economic rights (e.g., economic facilities, social opportunities, and protective security).[10]

In the United States, we generally limit our concept of rights to those negative restrictions on governmental power that have their sources in the Constitution. "Congress shall make no law abridging . . ." is the paradigm. But there are movements from all points along the political spectrum for a more expansive, positive view of rights. Many on the right, and even in the center, favor a constitutional amendment establishing the rights of crime victims. Some on the left advocate a right to affirmative action based on race or gender. Some see health care, education, and safety as rights. Others advocate welfare, or at least a minimum subsistence, as a right.

In addition to these genuinely positive rights, a novel and dangerous "vocabulary of rights" is being constructed as part of an attempted end run around the Constitution. "Victims' rights," the "right to be protected from pornography," "fetus rights," and the "right not to be exposed to secular humanism" are elements of a jargon conceived by right-wing groups to deceive the public into believing that an invocation of governmental power is really an exercise of individual rights.

Rights—especially constitutional rights—exist in relation to governments. The Bill of Rights (and post–Civil War amendments) was designed to limit governmental powers by assuring that certain individual rights could not be taken away by representatives of the government. In the context of criminal prosecutions, the defendant or suspect was given the right to be free from compelled self-incrimination, double jeopardy, cruel and unusual punishment, and excessive bail.

There is no provision for victims' rights in the Constitution for the simple reason that it is not usually the government that seeks to deny the victim any legitimate claim.[11] The victim was assaulted by a private citizen. The government is on the side of the victim and is prosecuting the defendant. The Bill of Rights seeks to strike a balance by granting the defendant certain rights. In practice, however, the government does not always work in the interest of victims, especially when they are poor, unpopular, or powerless. Even middle-class victims are often neglected, inconvenienced, or abused. Understandably, therefore, victims'-rights lobbies have been formed that seek for victims a greater role in the criminal-justice system. These groups have become the darling of prosecutors and politicians. How can any decent citizen resist the emotional importuning of crime victims? Prosecutors no longer claim to be representing the impersonal government (the same one that takes your hard-earned money and doesn't answer your letters). Now they are champions of victims—a group with which every citizen whose home has been burgled or pocketbook snatched can identify.

Legislatures have also jumped on the victims'-rights bandwagon. More than half of our states have enacted victims'-rights laws. Most of these laws are the old wine of law-and-order legislation in a new bottle. Some contain few or no real protections for victims: They simply take rights away from defendants. Other legislation does improve the situation for victims and witnesses by eliminating certain inconveniences and requiring that their interests be taken into account by those who administer the criminal-justice system.

Among the most controversial provisions of these new laws is the right of the victim—or the victim's representative—to appear before the sentencing judge and the parole board and to present a victim-impact statement. These statements provide parole boards and sentencing authorities with emotional and highly detailed accounts of how the crime actually affected, and continues to affect, the victim. While there may be some value in humanizing the process by pitting defendant against victim instead of the impersonal prosecution, a victim-impact statement carries with it considerable cost. It invites class and race biases. When the victim is someone with whom the sentencing authorities can identify, they are apt to see the crime as more serious and deserving of harsh punishment than when the victim is poor, homeless, unemployed, or a member of an unpopular group. The status of the victim has long been known to have a demonstrable impact on the severity of the punishment, but the increasing visibility of the victim in the criminal-justice process threatens to exacerbate this discrimination. The concept of victims' rights is clearly a knife that cuts both ways.

The Supreme Court has issued conflicting rulings on this issue over the years, but the victims'-rights movement is stronger than ever and the rhetoric of victims' rights is likely to persist in many contexts. So-called victims of pornography will continue to parade through the streets demanding their "right" to have the government remove offending material from their communities. Graphic photographs of "abortion victims" are commonplace at right-to-life demonstrations. Christian fundamentalists are declaring themselves victims of secularism, claiming a right to have the government support religion and restrict the teaching of evolution in public schools.

Those right-wingers who are using this new rhetoric of rights in an effort to undermine the rights of the individual are misusing words in a deliberately confusing manner. The concept of rights in relation to governmental powers is too important a part of our national identity to be obscured by such faddish rhetoric. I have come across so many claimed rights that I thought it might be useful to list some of them, along with the claimed counterrights.

Right	Counterright
Right to life of fetus	Right to choose abortion
Right to life of dying person	Right to assisted suicide
Right not to be executed	Right to have loved one avenged
Right to be well fed	Right of animals not to be eaten
Right to keep and bear arms	Right to safe streets
Right of criminal defendants	Right of victims
Right to free speech	Right not to be offended
Right to keep one's money	Right to equitable distribution of wealth
Right-to-work law	Right to collectively bargain
Right to sexual privacy	Right to a moral society
Right to influence elections by voters	Right to equality of contributions
Right to be a free agent in sports	Right of team to continuity
Right of employee to a four-day work week	Right of employer to labor of work-week employee
Right to privacy and anonymity	Right to know who is criticizing you on the Internet
Right to confidentiality (lawyer, minister, doctor, rape counselor, etc.)	Right to subpoena relevant information
Right of parents to control access to children	Right of grandparents to visit grandchildren

Parental right to remove child from school for religious reasons	Right of child to education and to choose different life
Right of parent to refuse medical treatment for child on religious grounds	Right of child to live and choose different religion
Right of parent to discipline harshly	Right of child to be free from abuse
Connubial rights of husband	Right of wife to refuse
Right to smoke	Right not to be subjected to secondhand smoke
Right to clean environment	Right to a job that would be eliminated by environmental concerns
Right to a bilingual education	Right to linguistic uniformity
Right to an organ from dead	Right of person to be buried with organs
Right of parents to know of underage daughter's abortion	Right of daughter to choose abortion without parents knowing
Right to choice of doctors	Right to equal medical care
Right not to be tested for DNA	Right to evidence of innocence
Right to build a church, synagogue, or mosque in neighborhood	Right to residential control
Right to fair housing practices	Right to live in homogeneous neighborhood
Right to proselytize	Right to be free from proselytization
Right to treatment	Right to refuse treatment
Right to confidentiality of tax information	Right to relevant information
Rights of animals	Rights of humans to use animals for medical experimentation
Right to genetic privacy	Right of insurer or employer to assess risks
Right of defendant to have victim's body disinterred for DNA testing	Right of victim's family to peace for victim's body
Right of rape victim to have defendant tested for sexually transmitted diseases	Right of defendant to presumption of innocence and privacy
Right of rape victim to have her identity undisclosed	Right of defendant to disclose name of alleged victim in order to elicit challenge to her credibility
Right of gay couple to adopt	Right of child to be adopted by heterosexual family
Right to quote from and parody any written work	Copyright of author
Right of owner to alter art	Right of artist to integrity of his art
Right to know of sex offenders in neighborhood (Megan's Law)	Right of privacy after serving sentence
Right to your name and identity	Property right in domain names fairly purchased

Right to prevent stranger from changing his name to yours	Right to choose an identity
Right to express sexist, racist, homophobic, and other bigoted views	Right to be free from hostile environment
Right to jury nullification	Right to equal protection of law
Right to procreate without limits	Right to live in an uncrowded world
Right to borrow money without excessive interest	Right to make profit on risk
Right to refuse to testify against your child, parent, spouse, friend, etc.	Right to everyone's testimony
Right to a hand recount of machine votes	Right to a final machine vote without "subjective" recount
Right to be free from racial or ethnic profiling	Right to be safe from hijackers and other criminals
Right to anonymity	Right to be protected from identity theft by a foolproof national identity card

The difficult question is whether it is wise to "constitutionalize" so many areas of what have traditionally been deemed matters of politics and policy. To constitutionalize a preference into a right is to remove it from majoritarian determination and to turn it over to unelected judges (at least in the federal system) for judicial review.

The power of judicial review has itself derived its legitimacy from the experiences of our people over time. It has become an important component of liberty, though—like other components—it is subject to abuse and misuse.[12]

Rights play an essential but limited role in a democracy, most importantly as a check on majority rule. It follows that not every strongly held preference should be recognized as a right. In a democracy, majority rule must remain the default position. Unless it can be shown convincingly that a claimed right is necessary to prevent serious wrongs, majority rule should prevail. The proliferation of claimed rights not only trivializes those fundamental rights that have proved their value from experience, it endangers democratic governance itself. Rights are not right unless they prevent wrongs.

CHAPTER 15

Is There a Right "to Life"?

THE DIVISIVE DEBATE over the "right to life" well illustrates the intellectual bankruptcy of claims based on natural or divine rights. Reasonable, intelligent, and moral people fundamentally disagree about whether, when, and to what extent a pregnant woman or girl should have the right to choose to have an abortion rather than to choose to give birth. There is nothing in the nature of man or woman that definitely resolves this issue,[1] nor any definitive logical argument that leads inexorably to one or another conclusion. Neither is there an unequivocal biblical commandment, as evidenced by the fact that believers in the Bible disagree about the abortion issue.*

Some arrogantly proclaim that if people only thought more clearly and morally, they would all understand that abortion violates the natural right of the living fetus. Others argue that if people thought more logically, they would all understand why compelled birth violates the natural rights of the mother. Both are demonstra-

---

*If human birth were like kangaroo birth, the arguments regarding abortion might well be different. Kangaroo fetuses are "born" earlier in the process of gestation. "Joeys" emerge from their mothers' internal womb after only five weeks, but immediately return to a more external womb—the pouch—where they continue the process of gestation for an additional forty-two weeks. If human birth were similarly segmented, birth would be seen more as a process and less as an absolute point of demarcation as to when life begins.

bly wrong, since clear-thinking, moral people come to diametrically opposite conclusions based on their differing worldviews, values, upbringings, experiences, and assessments of the future.[2] Each side may well be right, if one accepts the premises of its arguments. Some of the premises are plainly empirical; for example, easy abortion promotes sexual promiscuity.[3] Others are plainly faith-based; for example, God has ordained that no abortions—or only some abortions—may be performed. Still other views purport to be based entirely on moral claims without regard to facts—but upon analysis, they turn out to have a significant empirical component; for example, if abortion is permitted, it will diminish the value we place on human life and make it easier for us to justify other takings of human life. This sort of slippery-slope argument is premised on empirical claims that may be difficult to establish, but they are empirical claims nonetheless.

For many, experience is the determining factor in the abortion debate. They look to the experience of countries that have prohibited all abortion, and they see young women who have been killed or injured by illegal abortionists performing surgery in back rooms without proper medical care. They see the hypocrisy of the rich being able to secure medical abortions in other countries while the poor are denied that option. They see the difference between preserving the life of an eighteen-year-old sentient woman and preserving the opportunity for a month-old fetus to be born.

Experience also provides some support to the other side of the debate. As sonograms and other technologies make it clear that fetuses move, feel, and experience pain, the claim that they are "alive"—at least at a certain point in their development—becomes more compelling. The argument against late-term abortion (characterized by opponents as "partial-birth abortion") is also informed by experience with this procedure (really procedures) and by technological advances that permit a late-term fetus to be born alive and survive outside of the mother's womb.

As a consequence of these and other experiences, the discussion over abortion has become more nuanced and less absolute. As science develops earlier interventions into pregnancy—such as "morning-after" pills—and as science also permits the fetus to survive outside of the womb earlier in the pregnancy, the moral issues will be seen differently by many. There is surely a difference in degree, if not in kind, between a two-day-old embryo and an unborn but nearly fully developed fetus that can live outside of the womb. That difference will have a profound effect on the way the moral issues are seen by many nonideological people. Scientific developments will probably provide support for those who favor choice near the beginning of pregnancy, while also providing support for those who oppose abortion near the end of pregnancy. Many who believe that a pregnant woman should have the choice not to carry a fetus in her womb will not go so far as arguing that a woman whose late-term pregnancy can be terminated by the live extraction of the fetus (or baby) should have the right to end the life of that fetus (or baby). The continuing debate will increasingly focus on the middle period of pregnancy, when the fetus shows signs of being a life but is not yet able to survive outside of the womb. Experience will continue to shape the terms of the abortion debate.

Consider as well the debate over the morality of the death penalty. Some who favor abolition of the death penalty on religious grounds cite the commandment "Thou shalt not kill." Proponents read the commandment differently: "Thou shalt not *murder,*" arguing that execution of the guilty is not murder. They distinguish between the killing of an innocent fetus and the killing of a guilty criminal. Abolitionists point to the reality that any system of capital punishment will inevitably include some innocent defendants who were falsely convicted. Capital-punishment supporters respond that there is a difference between the deliberate killing of a person known to be innocent (like a fetus) and the inadvertent killing of a person erroneously believed to be guilty. They invoke the religious-moral concept of the "unintended effect," which allows an action to be taken if no immoral result is specifically intended, even if such an outcome is statistically inevitable.[4] (Some of these same moralists refuse, however, to distinguish between terrorists who deliberately target non-combatants and seek to maximize civilian deaths, on the one hand, and democratic nations that target only combatants but kill some non-combatants inadvertently, despite their best efforts to minimize civilian casualties. This is pure moral hypocrisy motivated by a political result-oriented double standard.)

Those who oppose the death penalty but favor a woman's right to choose abortion offer yet another distinction: An executed defendant—even a guilty murderer—is a human being, whereas a fetus is not a human being.[5] For them, innocence or guilt and willfulness or inadvertence are not the determining issues. The issue is the humanity of the person executed versus the non-humanity of the fetus.*

In my criminal-law classes on capital punishment, I begin by asking how many students categorically oppose the death penalty on moral grounds alone (killing guilty murderers is wrong in and of itself, even if it deters), rather than on empirical grounds (capital punishment does not deter, some innocents are mistakenly executed, it is unfairly applied, etc.). About half the students raise their hands. I then challenge them: What if I can persuade you that the death penalty—as contrasted with life imprisonment—does, in fact, deter the murder of one innocent potential victim for every guilty

---

*But remember the kangaroo! With modern technology, first-trimester fetuses may someday be able to "live" outside of the mother's womb. How will the debate then change?

murderer who is executed? A few hands go down. What if every execution deters ten murders? More hands go down. What if we could avoid mistakes? Apply the death penalty fairly? Even more hands go down. I persist: How can you justify, on moral grounds, preferring the lives of guilty murderers over those of innocent victims? If you do, don't you become complicit in immorality? Is there really a moral difference between actively killing the guilty and passively allowing the innocent to die because of your deliberate inaction? A few determined hands remain raised. The point of the exercise is to demonstrate that moral arguments are often implicitly based on empirical assumptions. If the facts change—if experiences differ—then the moral conclusions change, at least for some.

Not every moral person sees the debate over capital punishment in absolute, either-or terms. Some strongly believe that there is a difference between executing a mass murderer who shows no remorse—such as Timothy McVeigh—and a rehabilitated situational murderer like Karla Faye Tucker.* Others, such as John Kerry, oppose the death penalty except for terrorism. The Catholic Church generally opposes capital punishment except when the death penalty is the only means of protecting other innocent lives.

These, and other, nuanced views are the result not of a priori assumptions, but of experience with the actual administration of capital punishment. The recent development of DNA testing, and the resulting vindication of claims of innocence by many who were sentenced to death, have changed minds. So has the statistical demonstration of racial bias in the imposition of the death penalty.

---

*Karla Faye Tucker was twenty-three years old when she and her boyfriend bludgeoned two people to death. She admitted to her part in the killings, stating that they gave her sexual gratification. She was sentenced to death. While awaiting her execution, Tucker said she underwent a religious conversion. She accepted Christianity and worked in a prison-based ministry. Citing the fact that Tucker was a born-again Christian, and now a different person, many advocated sparing her from the death penalty. She was ultimately executed by the state of Texas in 1998.

My point here is not to resolve either the capital punishment or the abortion debate. It is to demonstrate how the terms of these debates can be influenced by how the issues are framed, how the premises are articulated, how the level of discourse is selected, and whether we look to experience or to external sources for our rights. It is also to demonstrate that invoking a divine or natural "right to life" is not an argument. It is a cliché.*

---

*The right to life is also invoked by all sides of the debate over stem cell research. Advocates point to its life-saving potential, while opponents argue that the use of stem cells will diminish the value of life.

CHAPTER 16

Is There a Right Not to Be Censored by Government?

T HE RIGHT NOT to be censored by the government is an example of a right that can be derived by our experience with wrongs. It certainly does not come from God, whose spokesmen often claim a monopoly on truth. Nor does it derive from nature, since censorship has been the norm for thousands of years. Experience has shown that empowering the sovereign to be the judge of all truth—as Hobbes proposed—leads to terrible wrongs. That is why the American constitutional experiment denied the government this historic power.

The paradigm of an American right is the guarantee of freedom of speech under the First Amendment to the Constitution. But contrary to popular opinion, that amendment bestows no general right on Americans to say what they please under all circumstances. Any discussion of freedom of speech in the United States must first clarify its scope under the positive law of our Constitution. There is no right to speak freely in all contexts. If you say something your boss does not like, he may fire you. Your spouse may leave you. Your parents may punish you. Your private school may expel you, and your friends may abandon you. Only *the government* may not restrict your right of free speech.

The reality is that our Constitution grants few affirmative rights, such as freedom of speech. What it does do—especially through the

Bill of Rights—is to restrict the power of government to engage in certain activities, such as censoring speech or the press.

Illustrative of this common mistake was a *Boston Globe* column on February 1, 2000, by Bob Ryan on the decision by Major League Baseball to suspend pitcher John Rocker for making bigoted remarks in an interview. This is what Ryan wrote:

> Has anyone in Major League Baseball ever heard of the United States Constitution, the First Amendment of which, as every high school civics student is supposed to know, pertains to free speech?
>
> This is a wonderful country, not in the least because it allows freedom of expression to all its citizens, drawing the line at such things as advocating the violent overthrow of the government. . . .
>
> [Rocker] is protected by more than just Voltaire's rhetoric. He is—or, at least he should be—protected by the Constitution of the United States of America. What makes America great is that the John Rockers of the world have every right to stand up and reveal their essential ignorance, just as we have every right to rebut each of their outrageously uninformed viewpoints. . . . An acid tongue is protected by the Constitution. . . . Trampling constitutional rights we hold dear is not the answer.

In a *New York Times* op-ed piece the next day, I wrote the following:

> Despite the common myth that we can say anything we please in this country, the fact is that our Bill of Rights does not grant Americans any general right of free speech.
>
> That's why Bud Selig, the baseball commissioner, can suspend and fine John Rocker, the Atlanta Braves pitcher, for expressing bigoted views in a magazine interview.
>
> Indeed, when announcing the suspension on Monday, Selig said that Rocker "brought dishonor to himself, the Atlanta Braves, and Major League Baseball."

But to conclude that baseball has the right to suspend Rocker does not mean that it was right to do so.

The First Amendment prohibits "Congress" and, by modern interpretation, federal and state governments from "abridging the freedom of speech, or of the press." The amendment, then, is a restriction on government power, not a right to say anything without fear of all consequences. The First Amendment says nothing about the power of private employers, universities, or sports leagues to censor or punish speakers who express views with which they disagree.

Thus, Selig was well within his rights as the chief executive of a private corporation to make an independent decision to suspend Rocker.

The problem is that his decision violates the *spirit* of free speech that animates the First Amendment. The Constitution may impose limits only on the government, but the First Amendment is premised on the idea that there should be a free marketplace of ideas. Private universities, for example, are not constrained by the Constitution, but most choose to follow it anyway, because they recognize that the exchange of ideas— no matter how wrongheaded or obnoxious—is good for education.

By accepting this model of open discourse, no university can reasonably claim to be "dishonored" by views expressed by students or faculty members, since they do not reflect the collective thinking of the university.

Baseball is not, of course, a university, and diversity of views is not essential to the enterprise. But trash talking, banter, razzing, and taunting have always been part of the game. However offensive his comments, Rocker had every right to insult New York and New Yorkers. He crossed a line when he moved to racist and ethnic stereotyping, but he is surely not the first player to have expressed such views. Will baseball now need a platoon of speech cops monitoring players in bars and at barbeques? Or will the new rule be limited to published comments? What about taunts on the field? Now that baseball has drawn a line in the sand, it must apply it uniformly.

Selig would have been wiser not to suspend Rocker but to announce that the league is committed to freedom of speech and that the
comments of individual players should not be misunderstood as re-
flecting the opinions of major-league baseball.

Such an approach would deny John Rocker or any other player the
power to "dishonor" the game, while allowing major-league baseball to
honor the spirit of free speech.

Ryan was wrong about the scope of the First Amendment, but he
was certainly right about Voltaire, whose famous statement "I disapprove of what you have to say, but I will defend to the death your
right to say it" reflects the spirit of free speech.

Judicial opinions have interpreted the Fourteenth Amendment—
which provides that the states may not deprive any person of "life,
liberty, or property, without due process of law"—as a broadening
of the First Amendment to include restrictions on the states and on
all official governmental actors, such as presidents, governors, public universities, and so on. Still, the First Amendment applies—explicitly—only to what is called "state action," that is, any action by
the government or someone acting on its behalf.

The question of freedom of speech raises a broader, more general issue about the nature of rights. The American concept of
rights tends to be negative: The government is denied the power to
restrict certain activities; the individual thus has a right, but only in
relation to the government. Freedom of speech, important as it is,
is largely a negative right. It is fair to ask whether it should also become a positive right. Is there a positive theory of free speech? Can
one be built on experience, especially our experience with the
wrongs of censorship?

There is considerable controversy over positive theories of free
speech: Is the search for truth facilitated by a wide diversity of
viewpoints being expressed in an open marketplace? Does the mar-

ketplace of ideas really work, especially in a world in which the marketplace is heavily skewed in favor of those who can afford to buy time in the media? There is considerable empirical evidence for the proposition that watching, listening to, or reading certain news media actually results in believing things that are demonstrably false.[1] The experiential case *for* freedom of speech is not nearly as convincing as the case *against* governmental censorship. Societies in which citizens do not choose to speak out publicly on a range of issues can be good and decent, if somewhat boring, places. There is far less public controversy in some Scandinavian countries than in the United States and some other European countries. Yet there is no less freedom, justice, or fairness in these "quiet" places than in more "noisy" venues. The same cannot be said about societies in which a system of governmental censorship determines what a citizen may say, write, read, or hear. It has been said that governments that begin by burning books end by burning people. This may overgeneralize the historical record, but it makes an important point: A regime of governmental censorship often entails other evils, such as informers, searches, loyalty oaths, coercion, and torture—all of which are easier to hide in a regime of censorship.

Even without these additional consequences, the dangers inherent in governments dictating what their citizens can read, see, and hear are demonstrated by the historical record. The road to injustice has often been paved by governmental control over information. On the basis of this experience, we have developed a consensus, not necessarily about the *virtues* of free speech but about the *vices* of a regime of governmental censorship, especially prior restraint.

Our Bill of Rights does not entrench a general right of free expression: Corporations, universities, churches, families, and other nongovernmental entities need not allow their members to speak freely. Only the government may not "abridge" the freedom of speech by state censorship. Building on that core right, which grows out of our experiences with injustice, we are involved in a never-ending debate about its appropriate scope: Should it be permissible for a government to impose spending limitations on the exercise of free speech by the wealthy in order to level the political playing field for the less affluent? Does "pure" political speech deserve a higher level of constitutional protection than commercial or sexual speech? Should it be permissible for a government to censor certain genres of speech—for example, pornography, racism, and historical untruths—in the interests of promoting equality or some other social good? These and other proposed exceptions are being debated by reasonable people. Some opponents of such exceptions argue, in similar fashion to those who argue for a high wall of separation between church and state, that any governmental power to censor is wrong in and of itself, while others contend that it is the first step toward a full regime of censorship. Again, we need not await the development of a fully articulated positive theory of free expression. We can build a core right from the bottom up, based on the widespread consensus against governmental regimes of censorship that have contributed to the injustices of the past.

Justice Robert Jackson, in the middle of the horrors of the Second World War, drew some basic conclusions about rights from such experiences, in words with which few will disagree:

> If there is any fixed star in our Constitutional constellation, it is that no official, high or petty, can prescribe what shall be orthodox in politics, nationalism, religion, or other matters of opinion or force citizens to confess by word or act their faith therein.

This is a solid experiential foundation on which to build a more complete theory of expressive rights, as well as other fundamental rights.

Today, there is considerable debate about the "limits" of free speech in the age of terrorism. Does it include religious incitement to terrorism, of the kind heard weekly in mosques throughout the Middle East and other parts of the world? Should international tribunals, such as the one for Rwanda, be empowered to prosecute radio stations that issued instructions for conducting genocide?

There is also discussion about placing limits on the right of privately owned media conglomerates to take sides in elections. Should the American media, especially television, be subject to some "fairness" or "equal time" requirements?

The development of the Internet and our experiences with this powerful information system have also raised important new questions: How can defamation and violations of privacy be regulated in a transnational medium that encourages anonymity and that has no responsible "publisher"?

These are only some of the recent experiences that inform arguments over the limits of free speech. They will not be resolved any time soon, since we lack a coherent positive theory of freedom of expression that is widely accepted. In the meantime—and in life all of time is the meantime—we can build a compelling, if not absolute, right against governmental censorship based on our widespread experience with the grievous wrongs produced when governments are empowered to dictate what we can say, read, and ultimately believe.

CHAPTER 17

Is There a Right to Have Church and State Separated?

THE SEPARATION OF church and state is another example of a right based on experiences with wrongs. Reasonable people can and do disagree about what the ideal relationship between these institutions ought to be: Should governments be entirely neutral toward all religions and toward religion in general? Should the state discriminate against religious speech in the public forum? Should government agencies work with religious institutions on such common goals as the elimination of poverty and the reduction in teen pregnancy and sexually transmitted diseases?

The lessons of history tell us little about the ideal relationship between church and state, but they are relatively clear about the worst relationship: When the state establishes one particular religion and backs the religious ideology of that church with the military, police, and economic power of the government, this relationship corrupts religion and denies citizens freedom of conscience and the free exercise of religious choice. The results have been crusades, inquisitions, persecution of "witches," and state-sponsored religious terrorism.

This historical experience has led to a broad consensus—among many church leaders, government officials, civil libertarians, and moral philosophers—that government should not establish a particular church and support its particular religious ideology by force or finance; nor should it deny individuals the free exercise of their own religion, even if that religion is deemed to be "false" by the majority of citizens. (Strictly speaking, the right to have church and state kept separate is as much an institutional part of our broad system of checks and balances as it is an individual right, but our experience has shown that the individual right of religious freedom is so intertwined with the separation of church and state that we properly think of them as elements of a single package.)

From this bottom-up conclusion, arguments can and have been made about the content of the rights that should derive from the experiences of the world with the relationship between church and state. Building on these experiences, some argue that a high wall of separation must be placed between the "garden" of the church and the "wilderness" of the state. This powerful metaphor has animated much of the debate about freedom of religion and freedom from religion, which are two sides of the same coin. (Madison and Jefferson understood—far better than Bush and Falwell—that without freedom from religion there can be no freedom of religion, since for the religious zealot there is only one true religion and anything else is heresy.) Strict separationists argue that the wall of separation should preclude governments from supporting religion (in general) over secularism, even if they support no particular religion. Some believe that it is wrong, in and of itself, for a state to place its imprimatur on religion as such, while others believe that to do so is the first step down the slippery slope of establishing, or preferring, a particular religion.

Lurking in the background of this debate are the powerful images of Joan of Arc being burned at the stake, Galileo being sentenced to house arrest and forced to renounce his heliocentric theory, Jews being expelled from Spain and England, Jesus being crucified. These terrible experiences produce a consensus that every person should have the right to choose a particular religion, or no religion, without fear of state-supported persecution or discrimination. They also inform the debate over how high to build the wall of separation.

This bottom-up approach has the virtue of beginning with a baseline consensus, grounded in the experiences of injustice, and leaving room for reasoned debate beyond that consensus. It need not await the development of a fully articulated theory of the right to live in a society in which church and state are kept entirely separate. It is always a work in progress, building on core experiences and changing with new experiences.

Among the new experiences that may inform the discussion about the proper relationship between church and state is the close association between religion and terrorism in some cultures. Theocratic states with access to weapons of mass destruction—such as Iran and Pakistan—pose considerable dangers, especially if their established religion is apocalyptic and its reward-punishment calculus relates primarily to life after death. The case for building a high wall of separation between the military power of the state and the religious power of the church, mosque, or synagogue has been strengthened in the minds of many by the new dangers posed by radical religious states with nuclear weapons.

Whatever the ideal relationship might be between religion and government in a utopian world, experience has shown that no religion should ever be empowered to enforce its doctrines through the military force of the state.

CHAPTER 18

Is There a Right to Emigrate and/or Immigrate?

To ILLUSTRATE THE experiential basis for valuing particular rights over others, consider the right to emigrate from a country and to move elsewhere. Many people would not rank the right to leave very high among basic human rights. Some would not consider it a right at all, since they would deem the obligation to remain in one's homeland more important. In the nineteenth century, the right to emigrate would have seemed almost treasonous to a nationalistic Frenchman. To be sure, some malcontents chose to emigrate to the United States or Canada, but they were not "real" Frenchmen.

To many Jews, however, because of their particular history and experience, the right to emigrate has always been of transcendent importance. The "wandering Jew" has escaped persecution by moving from country to country, sometimes voluntarily, other times as a result of being expelled. Because they had no homeland during the nineteen hundred years between their expulsion from Palestine by the Romans and the reestablishment of the State of Israel, and because they were generally not considered first-class citizens in their adopted countries, some Jews felt little nationalistic obligation to remain in the face of persecution. If so many had not exercised their right to emigrate from Europe to America, particularly at the end of the nineteenth and beginning of the twentieth centuries, even more of the Jewish community would have been murdered during the Holocaust.

Nor are Jews the only people who have felt the need to emigrate. The United States is mostly composed of people whose ancestors exercised a similar right in the face of famine, poverty, religious persecution, and tyranny. Moreover, the vast majority of those who have exercised that right—or their descendants—have benefited enormously from its exercise. We have been treated well by our host nation and have become an important part of it. As a nation of generally successful immigrants, we tend to recognize the importance of the right to leave one place and move to another. People who have never had to exercise that right, or who have exercised it less successfully, have a lesser appreciation of its importance. On the other hand, people who have been expelled from their homeland may value "the right of return" more highly than the right to leave, especially if they have been treated poorly by their host countries.

One reason the Arab–Israeli dispute has proved so intractable is that the Palestinians, who believe that they were expelled from their homeland, and who have often been treated badly by their host nations, claim the right to return. The Israelis, who were denied the right to a Jewish homeland for so many centuries, claimed the right to reestablish such a homeland, especially following the Holocaust. The law of return, which entitles any Jew in the world to apply for Israeli citizenship, is regarded as one of the most fundamental laws of the Jewish nation. Its perceived importance cannot be understood without considering the historical and experiential background of the Jewish people, especially the refusal of virtually every nation in the world—even the United States and Canada, which boasted of their status as nations of immigrants—to accept Jewish refugees during the Nazi era. Had the gates of other nations been open to Jews, millions could have been saved from Hitler's ovens, since the Nazis' original goal was to rid Europe of Jews. Many Jews believe that if the State of Israel had been in existence during the Holocaust, its open doors would have saved many.

Following the end of the war, England—which controlled Palestine—imposed rigid quotas on the number of Holocaust survivors who were allowed into Palestine. Many Jews died or were imprisoned trying to evade these quotas. It is entirely understandable, therefore, that among the first laws enacted by the new State of Israel was the law establishing a right of return. If, as Oliver Wendell Holmes Jr. observed, the "life of the law has been experience," then it becomes apparent why the Jewish people elevated the right of every Jew in the world to seek asylum in the Jewish state over the right of Palestinians to return to the land from which they left or were expelled. Now some young Israelis, who have never experienced the need to leave a hostile nation but who have observed the suffering of Palestinians, are seeking to abolish or limit the law of return. This is not surprising. Historical experiences are generational even within a given society.

The point here is not to argue the Israeli–Palestinian conflict but to illustrate how the unique experiences and memories of a people influence the way in which they perceive and value particular rights. The right to leave a country or return to it does not come from God or nature, despite competing biblical claims to the contrary. It cannot be deduced from the logic of democracy. It grows out of the specific experiences of particular people over time.

An example from American history can also be used to illustrate how rights change with experience and context. In 1776 many high-minded and moral New Englanders believed that among the most basic political rights was the right to separate from the mother country and establish an independent nation. Less than a century later, the descendants of these high-minded and moral New Englanders supported a bloody war to prevent Southern states from exercising a similar right.[1] The circumstances were, of course, very different, but that's the point. Different circumstances and experiences generate different conceptions of rights. Moreover, arguments about rights tend to be made at levels of abstraction that maximize their persuasiveness and minimize their inconsistency. For example, some of those who favored secession focused on the right of self-determination rather than on the right to own slaves, whereas many who opposed secession argued about its consequences for slavery.

Although the right to leave a country may seem quite different from the right to engage in homosexual conduct, they share a common source. In both cases, experience has dramatically changed attitudes about these claimed rights. The Bible deems male homosexuality an abomination. Many modern religious conservatives consider it ungodly, abnormal, deviant, sick, immoral, or even criminal. Many liberals consider it genetically determined, while others regard it as a morally neutral life choice. The moral evaluation of homosexuality has changed, and continues to change, over the years. The law, too, has changed. The Bible sanctions execution of men who have sex with other men. The laws of the New England colonies replicated the biblical punishments. Thomas Jefferson drafted legislation criminalizing sodomy. In the twentieth century, it was first a felony punished by imprisonment and then a misdemeanor rarely punished in practice. Now few Western societies regard private, consensual homosexual conduct between adults to be the appropriate concern of the criminal-justice system, though some anachronistic laws remained on the books until they were struck down by the U.S. Supreme Court in 2003. This change did not result from a change in God's wishes or from a different logical deduction or from some alteration in human nature. It was entirely a consequence of our changing experiences in regard to homosexuality and homosexuals over time. As more gay and lesbian people have "come out," we have seen them serve with distinction as teachers, soldiers, elected officials, and ministers. We have cheered for them on athletic fields, observed them with their children, and cried for them when they have been beaten or killed. It is far more difficult to persecute, or to stand idly by while others persecute, people we know and admire.

As a result of changing experiences with gay and lesbian friends, relatives, and neighbors, there is an emerging consensus in the United States in favor of equal basic rights to many governmental benefits. There is not yet a consensus regarding the right to marry. This is understandable in light of our lack of experience with gay marriage, which is still an abstraction to most Americans. As more and more gays marry and experience proves—as it will—that gay marriage poses no danger to the "sacred" institution of heterosexual marriage, we will see objections to gay marriage diminish. The trend is plainly in that direction. Young people—who have more personal experience with openly gay classmates, teachers, colleagues, and friends—are more favorable to gay marriage than older people.[2] Soon, most Americans will recognize that it is wrong to discriminate against gay and lesbian couples in the context of marriage. Recognition of this wrong will serve as a foundation for the right of gay and lesbian couples to marry.

Virtually every newly recognized right—whether it be the right to leave a country or the right to marry a person of the same sex—has been invented by human beings based on the wrongs they experienced or observed. This dynamic process will continue until the end of human experience.

CHAPTER 19

Do Animals Have Rights?

U NTIL NOW, WE have been considering fairly traditional rights that are recognized—at least to some
degree—by many contemporary democracies. In order to illustrate
the utility of the experiential approach to the future development of
new rights, let us turn now to a number of claimed rights that are
not yet widely recognized but that may become established as the
result of changing experiences. We begin with animal rights. Then
in the next chapter, we shift to the rights of dead people.

When we talk about animal rights, what exactly do we mean? Do
we mean that the animals themselves have rights, such as not to be
tortured? Or do we mean that human beings have the right not to
experience the torturing of animals? Whose right is it? And does it
really matter?

One of the first laws of the Bible prohibits the eating of animals
that are still alive (Genesis 10:4). The Bible also prohibits human
beings from copulating with animals (Exodus 21:19, Leviticus
17:23). These rules would seem to be designed for the protection
of vulnerable animals, but another rule requires the execution of
the nonconsenting animal with which a man or woman has copu-
lated (Leviticus 20:15–16). Animal sacrifices are also mandated
throughout the Bible, along with humane slaughter laws. Taken
together, these rules appear to be largely ritualistic, designed more

to keep human beings pure and holy than to protect the rights of animals. Indeed, the Bible explicitly declares that humans should "rule over" the animals, and that the animals are "given into" the hands of humans (Genesis 1:28, 9:2).

In theory, a divine- or natural-law approach could include rights that inhere in animals, since rights come from an external source— God or nature—that could bestow them on any being or object. God could grant rights to trees, rivers, forests, or rocks.[1] Nature could be as inclusive as those who purport to interpret it choose to be. Positive law, too, could enact rights for nonhumans, but any such rights would be the product of human decision-making. It would be human beings who decided to extend rights beyond their own species.*

There are other examples—none completely analogous—in which those in a position to create rights bestowed them on others who were not part of the rights-granting process. Benevolent despots have granted limited rights to their nonvoting subjects, as have slaveholders to slaves, male voters to female nonvoters, adults to children, the mentally competent to the incompetent, and so on. Even though the recipients of these rights did not participate in the process that bestowed them, the rights *belonged* to the subjects, the slaves, the females, the children, and the incompetent, who had standing to invoke them even against their superiors. As Alice said, "a cat may look at a king."

We can understand the concept of rights as applied to other human beings, even if we treat them as subordinates politically, legally, and in other ways. But it is far more difficult to think about

---

*The Roman emperor Caligula, whom history has portrayed as a mad tyrant, reportedly planned to elevate his favorite horse to the position of consul, a very high political post. One historian dismisses the story as a mere "famous rumour," however. H. H. Scullard, *From the Gracchi to Nero: A History of Rome from 133 B.C. to A.D. 68* (London: Routledge, 1996), pp. 283–285.

rights as applied to nonhumans. When we say, metaphorically, that trees, rivers, and forests have rights, we plainly mean that human beings have rights in relation to their preservation. Our grandchildren and great-grandchildren, who are not yet here to express their wishes, have the right to be left a planet that is not polluted or otherwise destroyed. That is *their* human right, as it is ours, but it does not belong to any particular tree, river, or forest. (Nor does it belong to any particular human being, born or unborn.)

Animals are different from rivers. They suffer, they feel, they fear, they remember. At least, some of them do. As Oliver Wendell Holmes Jr. once observed, "Even a dog distinguishes between being stumbled over and being kicked." We can understand the statement "a cat has the right not to be tortured" far more readily than we can give meaning to the argument that "a tree has the right not to be cut up into small pieces." As sentient beings, we can identify with the pain and fear of a tortured animal. But does that mean the animal has (or should have) a right not to be tortured? Or merely that we, as humans, have the right to live in a society that does not tolerate the torture of animals?[2] (Another, even more pragmatic human-centered approach to the prohibition against torturing animals might be based on the empirical assertion that permitting the torture of animals might encourage violence against human beings, or that those who torture animals are more likely to move on to human victims.)[3]

It does make a difference how we think about this right, perhaps not so much in the context of gratuitous torture—which would be prohibited under any reasonable theory—but surely in the context of eating animal flesh, wearing their skins, and experimenting with their bodies. If the right belongs to the animal itself, then we must ask why we are (or should be) permitted to kill an animal for our culinary or fashion pleasure if others are not permitted to torture them for their more perverse pleasure. (If animals had the right not to be killed, would that obligate humans to try to prevent lions from eating sheep?) If the right belongs to human beings, then there may be a stronger argument for balancing it against human needs and desires, such as good nutrition, a tasty meal, a fashionable coat, or a cure for a human disease. But if the right belongs to the animal itself, how can we, who vote, strike the appropriate balance between our needs and the right of the animal, who doesn't get to vote on it?

There is also the theoretical question of where the rights of animals would come from. Surely there can be no social contract between humans and animals. The Kantian imperative and the Benthamite calculus appear to be limited to humans. How can animals be placed in John Rawls's "original position"? Any reference to nature would immediately deny animals all rights, since the law of the jungle is power-based, not rights-based. And it was God who ordained man's supremacy over the animals and his right to eat them (or at least some of them) and domesticate them, subject only to certain ritual limitations. Some of these ritual limitations imply a concern for the animal itself: rules of slaughter and the commandment requiring a day of rest for domestic beasts. But the object of these restrictions seems to be the humans on whom the limitations are placed, rather than the animals themselves. Indeed, most religious-based rights are human-centered precisely because humans are deemed to have souls and animals are not.* Those who advocate a more secular natural-rights theory might substitute the terms *consciousness* or *sentience* for *soul* but would still distinguish sharply between the rights of humans and those of other species.

For those who reject the categorical distinctions ordained by God or by the external mandates of nature, there can be no sharp

---

*Even the presence of a soul was once deemed scientifically provable, as a nineteenth-century pseudoscientist weighed dying people immediately before and after they died and their souls left them. He purported to come up with the precise weight of the human soul. He did not perform control experiments on dying animals.

natural line between humans and animals. We are on a continuum of soulfulness, consciousness, sentience, and capacity to feel fear and pain. Some animals are closer to the human end of that continuum than some human beings. Yet we insist on creating a separate category for *all* human beings. It is murder to willfully kill the most mentally impaired or permanently comatose human being, and it is not murder to kill the most educated and feeling primate or dolphin. We insist on maintaining (or constructing) this sharp dividing line because we fear the uncertainties of the continuum. Once we allow any member of our species to be treated as we treat any member of a "lower" species, we empower humans to make their own decisions about the "worth" of other humans. Constructing an absolute line is seen as a protection against the slippery slope. It serves as a fence protecting the core right of sentient human beings not to be murdered.

The dangers of a continuum approach to human worth are well illustrated by the history of our use and misuse of animals. In the beginning, animals were used to preserve human life. We needed their flesh to prevent us from starving, their skin and fur to protect us from freezing, and their bones as essential tools.* Today animals are still needed for human survival in some parts of the world, but in most places they mainly enhance the quality of life. We use them for testing cosmetics and other luxuries. We also use them for medical purposes, some potentially lifesaving, others life-enhancing. For many people, the lives of animals are simply not important. If we can use animals for *any* purpose, we can use them for *every* purpose—short of the infliction of gratuitous pain.

For some, drawing a line about the proper use of animals is crucial to leading a moral life, though they differ as to where the line

---

*Dangerous animals were also killed in self-defense. That still occurs, though on a smaller scale.

should be drawn. Strict vegetarians will eat no animal flesh, and even stricter vegans will consume no animal products. Some draw the line at mammals, or primates, or animals with "faces." Others will eat animal flesh but won't wear fur. Many will eat animals but not hunt them, while still others will hunt plentiful animals such as deer, but not scarce or endangered ones such as whales. Some favor animal experimentation for health but not cosmetic benefits. A small number of people oppose pet "ownership," preferring "guardianship." There are groups opposed to circuses, rodeos, horse and dog racing, zoos, and horseback riding. At the other extreme, there are proponents of cockfighting, bearbaiting, and even animal sacrifices. Many environmentalists oppose the clearing of rain forests, jungles, and other animal habitats to satisfy human needs. There are even those who argue that great apes should have human rights.[4]

Once we place the worth of animal life on a continuum, everything becomes a matter of degree. There are no natural criteria for where the appropriate lines should be drawn. It becomes largely a matter of personal taste. Human life can, of course, also be a matter of degree, as evidenced by the debates over when life begins and ends; whether it is proper to take the life of murderers or aggressors; when it is permissible to engage in just wars, proactive self-defense, and other life-and-death issues that have divided humankind over the millennia. But it is the near-universal view that human life has a high value, which may be balanced only against other high values. That is not the near-universal view regarding animal life. We certainly do not want humans to treat other humans in the way that we, as a species, have long treated animals.

To avoid this, we have made the somewhat arbitrary decision to single out our own species—every single member of it—for different and better treatment. Does this subject us to the charge of speciesism? Of course it does, and we cannot justify it except by the fact that in the world in which we live, humans make the rules. That reality imposes on us a special responsibility to be fair and compassionate to those on whom we impose our rules. Hence the argument for animal rights.[5]

The strongest case for animal rights derives from the history and experiences of human beings. Societies that treat animal life with greater respect tend also to treat human life with greater respect. It is preferable to live in a society that seeks to limit the suffering of animals than in one that does not. This does not necessarily mean that a vegetarian society will always be better than a carnivorous one. Hitler, it is said, was a vegetarian, and the Nazi SS surely treated their dogs better than they treated the Jews and Gypsies. Nor is it an argument against necessary medical experimentation on animals, since history and experience have shown that societies that take animal life to preserve human life can be good and caring places in which to live—at least for humans! It is merely a claim that the gratuitous infliction of pain on animals is bad for humans, and its toleration is bad for any human society. This is the soft case for a human-centered approach to animal rights. It requires that when human beings balance their perceived needs against the interests of animals, we must take into account their suffering and seek to minimize it (as we should take into account and try to minimize environmental damage when we create jobs and businesses).

This soft case for human-centered animal rights recognizes what decent human beings have been doing for millennia, and it postpones the ultimate decision about broad-based animal rights to a future time when our history and experience no longer make them necessary for human use as food, clothing, or experimental subjects. As we learn more about what animals experience, we may change our views with regard to their rights. It is certainly possible that in centuries to come our descendants—having very different experiences than we had—will have great difficulty understanding how decent people could have treated animals the way we do.

CHAPTER 20

Do Dead People Have Rights in Their Organs?

AT THIS POINT in our history, human beings have a right, recognized by law, to be buried along with their organs, even when these organs could be used to save the lives of other human beings. There may come a time in the future when people who are dying of organ failure may claim a right to use the organs of dead people. How would a moral society evaluate this claimed right? Before we seek to answer this question, it will be useful to look more broadly at the role of social institutions in dealing with human nature, particularly as it relates to the human body.

Law, religion, custom, tradition, and morality all share in common certain mechanisms for influencing and improving human conduct—for making it less "natural." These mechanisms are premised on the assumption that in the absence of external rules of conduct, most humans would tend to act selfishly (I define *selfish* to include family).[1] The rules are designed to discourage human beings from making individualized ad hoc decisions based on a selfish cost–benefit analysis of the particular situation confronting them. Instead, they impose on individuals the obligation to think more generally, more broadly, more categorically, more altruistically, and more communally—that is, more morally. These rules prohibit different categories of acts. Some prohibit core evils, such as the killing of innocent people. Others prohibit acts that are not in themselves immoral but that are thought to lead to core evils. Such prohibited acts include driving too fast or while drunk. Yet other rules seem designed simply to condition people to accept limitations—even artificial limitations—on their appetites or instincts. These include ritual restrictions on the eating of certain foods or the performance of certain ritually impure acts.

The rules of law, religion, and morality seek to make it more difficult to act on the instinct of selfish preservation of individual and family and to make it acceptable—indeed, obligatory—to act on the basis of a broader principle. The specific principle may vary, depending on whether one is a Kantian, a utilitarian (act or rule), a believer in the Bible, or a follower of any other set of rules, but the mechanism is similar: It requires you to act not as if yours were the only situation, but as if it were part of a principled set of mutually binding obligations.

Consider, for example, the issue of cannibalism. Start first with the eating of a human being who has already died. Absent the constraints of law, morality, religion, and so on, any rational starving person—say, a sailor in a lifeboat, a soldier lost in a jungle, an entire city besieged and surrounded—would not think twice about eating the fresh meat of a dead person, any more than he or she would think about eating the fresh meat of a dead animal. Some might argue that it is "natural" for human beings to be revolted by the thought of eating the flesh of fellow human beings, even if they were not responsible for their death. But throughout history and throughout the world, people have eaten dead humans. We are revolted by the thought because law, morality, and religion have conditioned us to become revolted. If we had grown up in a world in which the eating of human flesh was common, we would not be revolted by such a diet any more than by our diet of animal flesh. Perhaps someday when artificial food becomes an easy alternative, our great-grandchildren will be as disgusted by the prospect of eating the flesh of animals who were once alive as my grandparents and parents were revolted by the thought of eating certain dead animals such as pigs and lobsters.

Why, then, do we not eat human flesh? For some, the answer is simple: God has told us not to. But the gods of the Polynesians said it was permissible. What if our God had said it was permissible? Putting the same question at a different level of abstraction: Why did our God—or those who have purported to speak in his name— single out the flesh of humans as prohibited food? It seems a waste in a world in which so many are starving. Perhaps the answer lies in the slippery slope. If we would permit the eating of the flesh of someone who was already dead, we might be more inclined to kill them for their food value, just as we do with animals. So we create a prophylactic rule—or, to use the words of the Talmud, we build a fence around the core prohibition. The core prohibition is the killing of human beings; the fence is the prohibition against the eating of already-dead human beings.

Perhaps there is another core principle behind not allowing the eating of human flesh. Is it that somehow the human body is sacred? That it should never be used as a means toward the end of saving another human life? Surely the answer to those questions must be no, as evidenced by the fact that we do not prohibit the harvesting of body organs of dead human beings for transplantation into live human beings who might otherwise die for lack of a needed organ. In principle, what is the difference between "harvesting" the flesh of dead human beings to save the lives of other human beings and "harvesting" their other organs? It cannot be personal preference alone. If it were, I might personally reject the distinction, unless someone could make a persuasive argument in support. If I were dead, I would just as soon have my flesh eaten in order to save the life of another human being as have my heart or kidneys removed for transplant. I make no claim to ownership of my body once dead, as evidenced by the fact that I have signed on as an organ donor. If there were a place to sign on as a flesh donor, I would do that as well—unless a larger principle were at stake.

There is, of course, this difference between transplanting an organ and eating the flesh. The organ is generally needed to save life. There is a one-to-one correlation. Eating human flesh, on the other hand, could become an appetite rather than a necessity. Indeed, we accept the eating of human flesh when absolutely necessary to save life, as in shipwrecks and following the famous airplane crash in the Andes in 1972. We just don't want it to become routine. We might develop the same attitude toward organ transplants if people began to transplant the blue eyes of dead people for purely cosmetic reasons.[2]

Even—perhaps especially—when organs are needed to save lives, we properly worry that transplantation may encourage the killing of some human beings for their organs. Such practices are believed to exist in certain parts of the world even today, and we have built fences to protect the living from being killed for their organs. No moral, religious, or law-abiding person would order an organ if he knew someone would be killed to provide it.[3] If we chose, we could build an even higher fence: namely, prohibit the use of the organs of the dead, just as we prohibit the use of their flesh.

When organ transplantation first became possible, some religious groups made precisely that argument: The human body is sacred; it must be buried with all its organs; removal of any organ, even if necessary to save human life, is a desecration. That is no longer the position taken by mainstream religions, most of which now tolerate, or encourage, organ donation (some encourage only the receipt of organs, not their donation, but that is an unacceptably selfish moral position). Moral leaders should encourage their followers to think of their corpses as containing living recyclable parts. This change in perspective should be made in the interests of saving human life, thereby enhancing rather than diminishing its value. A dead body whose usable organs have been removed should become a symbol of respect for the living body. It is all a matter of how we view it and what we teach our children. There is nothing "natural" or "un-natural" about cutting up a dead body to give life to a live one, whether by using its heart or its flesh.

To encourage respect for the living, we mandate respect for the dead. It is not so much that a dead person has rights in his remains, as that the living have rights to see the bodies of their loved ones treated with respect. It is a crime to desecrate a cemetery or a corpse. We require our pathologists to perform autopsies in a dignified manner. We dispose of body parts with respect. Soldiers risk their lives to recover the bodies of their fallen comrades. We do all this not because it matters to the dead but because it matters to the living. We have learned the lessons of history, which teach that societies that disrespect the dead bodies and resting places of the deceased tend to devalue the living bodies—the lives—of their contemporaries. What constitutes respect—burying a body *with* its organs or *without* them—is a matter of education and nurture rather than divine law or nature. In some societies, respect for the dead requires that the body be taken to a remote hilltop so that its flesh may be consumed by birds of prey. The circle of life!

The same can be said about abortion. Some who argue against abortion say that if we trivialize the "death" of a living human fetus, it becomes easier to devalue the life of a baby, a mentally retarded person, a prisoner, a Jew, a black, an enemy, a stranger. Others argue that to compel a woman to bring an unwanted baby into the world devalues the life of the child and the welfare of the mother. Again, there is no one naturally correct answer for all moral people.

Another, less compelling example of a fence around the core violation would be in the prohibition against selling and trading ivory.

There's nothing wrong, in principle, with using the tusks of dead elephants. But once a trade in ivory becomes acceptable, live elephants will be killed for their tusks. Accordingly, we try to make ivory an immoral and illegal commodity.* Likewise with those who would try to make the wearing of animal fur unacceptable. Again, we can distinguish in principle between stripping the fur from dead animals and killing animals for their fur, but the lesson of history is that permitting the former will encourage the latter. Thus we see the same principle in operation once again: We impose a seemingly irrational prohibition against a harmless use of resources—the flesh of dead people, the tusks of dead elephants, the fur of dead animals—in order to discourage a violation of the core principle, namely, killing to secure these same commodities.

There are, of course, intermediate approaches. We could impose harsh punishments on those who kill elephants for their tusks while encouraging the use of tusks from elephants that died naturally. Experience would then show whether it is necessary to have a blanket prohibition on the sale (or use) of all tusks in order to prevent the killing of elephants. Or we could distinguish between the use of fur from animals specifically bred and raised for their fur and from animals in the wild. In the end, it will be experience rather than some abstract natural rule that will determine how high we need to build the fence in order to protect the core value.

The very concept of a fence is a recognition that rights are built on our experience with wrongs. It is this experience that cautions us about the dangers of the slippery slope—about the inclination of some people to take arguments to the limits of their logic and beyond. The great irony is that it is experience with moral relativism,

---

*Ivory, unlike food or transplantable organs, is not a necessity. It is a luxury. But for those whose livelihoods depend on securing and selling this luxury, the line between luxury and necessity blurs.

situational ethics, and continua that leads some to argue for absolutes and clear lines, and to pretend (or persuade themselves to believe) that these absolutes and lines come from God or nature.

The argument for absolutes and clear lines, rather than for continua, is a plausible one, based on human experience. It is played out regularly in our courts, as some judges read provisions of our Constitution as absolute prohibitions on governmental power, while others read exceptions and a rule of reason into these same provisions. Justice Hugo Black argued that the First Amendment's statement that Congress "shall make no law . . . abridging the freedom of speech" meant what it said: *No* law means *no exceptions*. Justice Felix Frankfurter argued for a rule of reason pursuant to which the government could make laws abridging certain genres of dangerous or offensive speech. When a government lawyer would argue for an exception, Black would take out his worn copy of the Constitution and read "Congress shall make *no* law . . . ," banging the table as he shouted the word "no." Frankfurter would then mock Black by opening his copy of the Constitution and reading the same words, except that he would bang the table when he shouted the word "congress," emphasizing the fact that the literal prohibition applies only to one branch of the federal government, not to the states or to the executive or judicial branches.

Black was a legal positivist and a pragmatist. He did not believe that the absolutes he insisted on came from God or nature. Instead, he thought the framers had decided to impose absolute prohibitions on certain governmental actions as a result of their negative experiences with judicial discretion and slippery slopes. Frankfurter placed greater trust in elite judges and in their ability to interpret constitutional prohibitions in a reasonable manner. Both were products of their own very different experiences, Black as a populist legislator, Frankfurter as an elitist professor.

The debate over whether absolute prohibitions or relative continua provide better protections against slippery slopes should be an empirical one that can be resolved by human experience rather than by the Delphic voices of God or nature.

Let us now try to apply the experiential approach to a specific set of questions relating to organ donation. A friend of mine recently died because he was unable to get a suitable heart for transplant. No healthy hearts were available at the time he needed his transplant, and so in order to remain alive he had to settle for the heart of a patient with hepatitis. The heart transplant worked, but my friend soon died of liver failure.

My friend, unfortunately, is among the large number of Americans who needlessly die each year because other Americans selfishly refuse to donate lifesaving organs after their own deaths. In the United States, there is a presumption against organ donation at death, which can be overcome only if the potential donor has made an affirmative decision to consent to having his or her organs removed upon death. In many European countries, the presumption goes the other way: All people are presumed to consent to the lifesaving use of their organs unless they explicitly take action to withhold consent. The result is that many more organs are available for transplant patients in European countries than in our own.

I can imagine few more selfish and immoral acts than insisting that your lifesaving organs must be buried with you so that worms can eat them, rather than allowing them to be used by other human beings to save their lives or to restore sight. Yet many Americans refuse to consent to organ donation upon death. A significant number justify their act of selfishness by reference to their religion. But what kind of religion would preach that it is wrong to help save lives by donating organs from a dead body? Religious leaders should be in the forefront, urging their followers to overcome their fears and superstitions and take the simple step that will directly save lives.*

But religious leadership alone will not eliminate the critical shortage of organs. We need to change the law. At the very least, we should move toward the European system of presuming consent in the absence of explicit withholding of consent. Even this shift of presumption may not produce enough organs. The time has come to raise the question of who owns a person's life-giving organs after that person has died. Do you have a right to have buried or cremated parts of your body that could keep other people alive? Would it violate the rights of dead people or their families for a state to pass a statute mandating organ removal and reuse after death? (There already are statutes requiring the removal and preservation of organs when autopsy is mandated for evidentiary purposes.) Would there have to be an exception for religious objection? These are questions we ought to begin debating. Improvements in medical technology require us to rethink old attitudes about our bodies after death. Treating the dead body with respect is an important element of humanity, but the forms of respect may vary. We as a society might well—and should—come to believe that retrieving organs that can then be kept alive and given to others is a proper way of showing respect.

When organ transplants first became feasible, many traditionalists objected—on moral and religious grounds—to playing God and tinkering with nature. Over time, attitudes changed, and almost nobody today *turns down* a lifesaving organ on religious or moral grounds. The Golden Rule—which is central to Judaism, Christianity, Islam, and other religions—requires that we treat our neighbors

---

*Recently another friend, a modern Orthodox rabbi and scholar, lost a son in a traffic accident. He not only arranged to have his son's organs distributed among many who needed them, he also became active in a group of Orthodox rabbis urging organ donation as a mitzvah—a religious obligation.

as ourselves. Anyone willing to *accept* a transplant must be willing to give their own organs. Religions that permit their adherents to receive transplants *must* permit them to donate organs, lest they be accused of hypocritically violating the Golden Rule. Perhaps an additional encouragement to transplant donation would be a rule excluding all adults who had not consented to donating their organs from receiving the organs of others. At least there should be a preference for those who were willing to donate organs.

Anyone who refuses to sign the box on the driver's license application, which constitutes consent to removal of organs after death, is either a coward, a fool, a knave, or a slave to superstition or religious fundamentalism. There is no softer way of putting this. It is simply wrong to waste the organs of the dead when they can be used to give life. It is understandable that some relatives of a crash or shooting victim would not be willing to consent to the removal of organs from the bodies of their recently deceased loved ones. But it is not understandable for an adult to refuse to consent in advance to the life-giving use of his own otherwise useless organs. We should make such selfishness unacceptable as a matter of morality and perhaps even as a matter of law.

Eventually our experiences with organ transplantation may move our society toward the recognition that there should be no right to refuse to have your organs harvested for lifesaving use after your death. There should, of course, be a right not to have your death accelerated in order to maximize the chances that your organs can most effectively be used. That should be a matter of choice. And there should, of course, be a right not to be killed in order to have your organs used to save the life of a more important or wealthier person. We might need fences around these core principles, but there is the danger that a fence built too high may endanger other core values.

Organ transplantation provides a good example of important values clashing with others. First there is the claimed value in preserving intact the bodily integrity of a dead loved one, or even the right of the dead person to dispose of his body as he chooses. On the other side of the ledger is the value of preserving the life of the person in need of an organ. Does a live person have the right to the organ of a dead stranger if that organ, and that organ alone, means the difference between life and death? What if the person in need of the organ is a scientist on the verge of curing cancer, the president of the United States, or a single mother of two children? Does their right to live—and our right to have them live—outweigh the right of the deceased to be buried with all his organs? Will it really make a difference if he is buried with one less kidney, no liver, or no heart?

Of course, much depends on how the issue is framed. Instead of describing the choice as between the life of the recipient and the wish of a dead person, it could be described as between the right of a human being to make important decisions about the disposition of his body and the power of the state to compel that person to violate his religious, moral, or aesthetic principles. Thus the framing of rights issues exerts a powerful influence on the moral and political debate, and can be used to tilt the debate toward a favored position. Some religious and political leaders are particularly adept at this, and advocates on all sides of contentious issues employ these framing tactics.

In general our society gives individuals considerable authority to direct the disposition of their property after their death, but this right is not without some limits. A husband may not completely disinherit his wife. Nor may he deny the government its statutory share of his property—namely the inheritance tax. A body is, of course, different from a bank account or even a valuable painting. Even with regard to a painting, however, there may be some limits. If a private person who owned an important collection of early Picasso paintings maliciously decided to have them destroyed upon his death, some societies—France, for example—would prohibit such a destruction of what is deemed a national treasure.* In the United States some privately owned buildings are declared historical landmarks and may not be destroyed, even if destruction is in the private financial interests of the owner. All governments assert the power of eminent domain over property needed for certain public purposes.

There may come a time when our collective experience with organ transplantation causes us to disregard (or give less weight to) the wishes of dead persons and their families if their organs could save lives. If experience shows that widespread organ retrieval saves numerous lives at little cost—psychic, moral, and financial—a consensus may emerge regarding lifesaving organs as "rightfully" belonging to those most in need of them. If that were to occur, many more people would probably begin to donate their organs and there would be less need for mandatory confiscation. But if there were still a shortage, a mandatory system might be considered.[4]

Experience could, on the other hand, move us in the opposite direction. It could turn out that more frequent organ transplantation produces negative consequences, such as hastening the deaths of sick people with needed organs, diminishing the value we place on the human body, discouraging research on other lifesaving techniques, or creating a caste system in which certain recipients are preferred over others. If that were to be our experience, then it might well reinforce current attitudes against having one's body "cut up" after death. The point is that there is no natural or divinely mandated way of showing respect for the human body. Deciding whether to regard the dead human body as an integral entity to be buried intact, rather than as an expired container for recyclable lifesaving organs, is very much a matter of experience. As experiences change, so do attitudes and so do rights—even rights as emotionally laden as the claimed right to be buried or cremated with one's organs intact.

---

*Franz Kafka's literary executor refused to follow Kafka's instructions to burn his unpublished manuscripts and instead had them published.

The Future of Rights

Does Experience Teach Us That Rights Can Survive Emergencies?

American history has been punctuated by occasional national emergencies during which important rights were temporarily suspended. Following the outbreak of the Civil War, President Abraham Lincoln empowered his generals to suspend the writ of habeas corpus. During the Second World War, President Franklin Delano Roosevelt ordered the detention of more than 100,000 Americans of Japanese descent. Other presidents and governors have also abrogated rights during perceived emergencies, sometimes invoking the common-law concept of "martial law." Generally, the courts have reviewed such assertions of emerging power, sometimes deferring to the executive, while other times constraining the exercise of such extraordinary power.

In 1971, I wrote an article summarizing our national experience with the suspension of rights during emergencies and predicting, based on these experiences, what the courts might do in the event of another dire emergency. This is part of what I wrote:

> While the courts have delivered opinions full of promise and prose about their majestic role during crises and the "irrepealable" nature of our fundamental safeguards, they have acted far more cautiously. And experience teaches us that what courts have in fact done in the past is

a far better guide to what we may expect from them in the future than is the rhetoric they have invoked.

What then could we reasonably expect from our courts if any American president during a period of dire emergency were once again to suspend important constitutional safeguards? Our past experiences suggest the following outline: The courts—especially the Supreme Court—will generally not interfere with the executive's handling of a genuine emergency while it still exists. They will employ every technique of judicial avoidance at their disposal to postpone decision until the crisis has passed. (Indeed, though thousands of persons have been unlawfully confined during our various periods of declared emergency, I am aware of no case where the Supreme Court has ever actually ordered anyone's release while the emergency was still in existence.) The likely exceptions to this rule of judicial postponement will be cases of clear abuse where no real emergency can be said to exist, and cases in which delay would result in irrevocable loss of rights, such as those involving the death penalty. Once the emergency has passed, the courts will generally not approve further punishment; they will order the release of all those sentenced to imprisonment or death in violation of ordinary constitutional safeguards. But they will not entertain damage suits for illegal confinement ordered during the course of the emergency.

When these strands are woven together, there emerges an approach to the limits of martial law that was encapsulated by Justice Holmes: martial law is not "for punishment," but rather "by way of precaution, to prevent the exercise of hostile power." This distinction between "punitive" and "preventive" law runs through the cases and has been echoed by many commentators. But no sharp line exists between punishment and prevention, as Blackstone recognized many years ago: "If we consider all human punishment in a large and extended view, we shall find them all rather calculated to prevent future crimes than to expiate the past." Practically speaking, the distinction means simply that the courts will tolerate preventive detention during an emergency but they will not approve the carrying out of any part of a sentence after the emergency has ended.

This prediction of "what courts will do in fact" may not, of course, prove entirely accurate. Important changes have occurred since the end of the Second World War. The Warren Court entered "political thickets" into which previous Courts had been reluctant to tread. . . . Civil rights organizations have proliferated and are better—though probably not well enough—prepared for their roles in the event of an emergency suspension of civil rights. And, most important, the Vietnam War and other recent events may have divided the country beyond any possibility of full repair; short of the threat of mass destruction, we will probably never again see an emergency that will bring the country together in a unanimous display of solidarity and patriotism such as that which accompanied our entry into the Second World War.[1]

I was wrong in predicting that we would never again experience an emergency that united us as did World War II. The terrorist attacks of September 11, 2001, were as uniting—at least initially—as Pearl Harbor. But there is an important difference between conventional wars and terrorist threats, and this difference is becoming more apparent as time passes. Conventional wars are generally of limited duration. One side eventually wins, victory is declared, and the emergency is over. With the end of the emergency comes a restoration of suspended rights. The threat of terrorism is never-ending. The emergency thus becomes a permanent state, and the rights that were suspended remain suspended indefinitely. We have little experience as a nation with this type of enduring emergency, and predictions based on past experiences are likely to be inaccurate.

In late June 2004, the United States Supreme Court issued a number of decisions growing out of the Bush administration's response to the terrorist attacks. These decisions provide some basis for assessing how rights may fare in the age of terrorism.

Before we get to the specifics of these decisions, it is necessary to summarize the approach to rights taken by the Bush administration in the wake of 9/11. No attempt was made to abridge the rights of all Americans. There have been no governmentally imposed restrictions on freedom of speech or dissent (though Attorney General John Ashcroft did warn "those who scare peace-loving people with phantoms of lost liberty" that they are giving "ammunition to America's enemies" and "aid[ing] terrorists"). Nor has there been any abridgment of the "right to bear arms"—a right particularly popular with the Bush administration.[2] There have been no general curfews, national ID cards, limitations on travel (except for the inconvenience of airport security procedures), or other across-the-board restrictions that would affect—and perhaps be resented by—large blocks of voters. The only people whose rights have been abridged have been aliens, visitors, foreigners captured in other countries, and a handful of Americans suspected of complicity with terrorism. Virtually all of these people are Muslims and Arabs. The administration's approach has been to deny "them" their rights in order to protect "us." This "them–us" dichotomy has proved popular with the general public and has generated little broad-based opposition to the emergency measures.

The three cases that were decided by the Supreme Court all involved "them": The *Rasul* case was brought by fourteen foreigners captured in Afghanistan during hostilities and detained in military custody at the Guantanamo Naval Base in Cuba; the *Hamdi* case was brought on behalf of an American citizen (Yasser Esam Hamdi was born in Louisiana in 1980 and moved with his family to Saudi Arabia as a child) who was captured in Afghanistan and detained in Charleston, South Carolina; and the *Padilla* case was brought by an American citizen who was arrested at Chicago's O'Hare Airport as a material witness and then detained in Charleston as an "enemy combatant" on suspicion that he was involved in a plot to manufacture and detonate a dirty bomb in the United States.

In each case, the government claimed the authority to detain these alleged enemy combatants—whether they are foreigners, residents, or citizens—until the hostilities are over, in other words indefinitely. It also claimed the authority to deny them basic due-process safeguards, including the right to counsel, the right to contest their guilt in an American court, the right to trial by jury, the privilege against self-incrimination, and the availability of the writ of habeas corpus.

Consistent with the prediction I made in 1971, the Supreme Court employed techniques of "judicial avoidance" to sidestep the broadest challenges to the authority of the president during an ongoing emergency. The justices did not "actually order . . . anyone's release." They ducked the issue posed by the *Padilla* case—whether an American citizen, who has been arrested on American soil and then designated an "enemy combatant" by the president, can be detained indefinitely without any kind of a trial—by ruling that Padilla's lawyers had brought his habeas corpus petition in the wrong court. They issued a narrow, but important, decision in the *Hamdi* case, holding that an American citizen, captured abroad but held in the United States as an enemy combatant, must "be given a meaningful opportunity to contest the factual basis for that detention before a neutral magistrate." But it then defined "meaningful opportunity" in a manner quite favorable to the military authorities, who are free to use hearsay evidence and to ignore the presumption of innocence and instead employ a rebuttable "presumption in favor of the government evidence"—in other words a presumption of guilt. They can also use a military officer as the "neutral judge," instead of an independent member of the judiciary. Reasoning that "the full protections that accompany challenges to

detentions in other settings may prove unworkable and inappropri-
ate in the enemy-combatant setting," the court permitted the government to employ watered-down protections that provide for
some judicial oversight but virtually assure that the military will
prevail in close cases.

More important than this largely symbolic victory for procedural safeguards was the court's concern with the government's position that Hamdi's detention "could last for the rest of his life,"
since this "unconventional war" might not be "won for two generations." The court reiterated the principle that "detention may last
no longer than active hostilities," but it recognized that this "understanding may unravel" in the face of the current conflict, which is
"unlike" other past conflicts that "informed the development of the
law of war." The court decided that it did not have to rule on the
broad issue of whether indefinite detention would be warranted
even after *active* combat has ended, because "active combat opera-
tions against Taliban fighters apparently are ongoing in
Afghanistan." The duration of such combat is, of course, almost entirely within the control of the government, which can turn it off
and on like a spigot, and thus control the duration of Hamdi's detention, as well as of others now in confinement. But the court
seemed to be suggesting that it would monitor this situation and if
it concluded that the active-combat phase was the tail wagging the
dog of detention, it might intervene.

In the final case, *Rasul,* the court addressed the broadest issue:
whether the fact that foreign fighters were being held in Guantanamo—an American naval base on land leased indefinitely from
Cuba—stripped United States courts of all jurisdiction to inquire
into the basis for the detention. The court ruled that American
courts had the power to issue writs of habeas corpus in cases of foreign fighters being held in Guantanamo. Its ruling was quite narrow,
focusing on the reality that by "the express terms of its agreement

with Cuba, the United States exercises complete jurisdiction and control over the Guantanamo Bay Naval Base, and may continue to exercise such control permanently if it so chooses."

In assessing these decisions, Professor Cass Sunstein of the University of Chicago said that the court decided them "in the narrowest possible fashion," focusing on "procedural safeguards" and leaving "key issues . . . undecided." Sunstein praised the court for its narrow focus, arguing that "minimalism has real attractions, perhaps above all in a period in which judges are forced to reconcile the demands of national security with the commitment to liberty."[3]

Minimalism, or gradualism, also has the virtue of allowing the court to wait until we have more experience with the relatively recent phenomenon of mass terrorism and our response to it. Striking the proper balance between preserving rights and fighting wrongs requires an understanding and assessment of our current experiences and an ability to translate these experiences into lessons for the future. This is a daunting task, especially with regard to rights, because rights should be built on a long view of experiences, rather than on an immediate reaction to temporary wrongs. For example, in the weeks leading up to the recent Supreme Court decisions, the media was saturated with the gruesome images of detainees being abused by American soldiers in the Abu Ghraib prison in Iraq. The justices were not oblivious to these images. They are part of our current experiences, and I would be surprised if they had no influence on any of the justices, as they obviously did on politicians, reporters, and members of the general public. But the responsibility of the justices is different from the responsibility of politicians or reporters. The justices, in defining and articulating rights, should be taking a longer view of wrongs. They should not be unduly influenced by the immediacy of these visible wrongs—any more than they should be unduly influenced by the searing images of the Twin Towers crumbling—though they cannot be expected to ignore them completely.

Placing current crises in a proper historical context is an important part of their job.

This longer historical perspective was reflected in the broad language of several of the justices, if not in their narrow rulings. Justice Sandra Day O'Connor, in writing for a plurality of the justices, noted that

> [i]t is during our most challenging and uncertain moments that our Nation's commitment to due process is most severely tested; and it is in those times that we must preserve our commitment at home to the principles for which we fight abroad.

Among these principles is the need for a judicial check on executive actions, even during times of emergency:

> We have long since made clear that a state of war is not a blank check for the President when it comes to the rights of the Nation's citizens. . . . But even the war power does not remove constitutional limitations safeguarding essential liberties. . . . Thus, while we do not question that our due process assessment must pay keen attention to the particular burdens faced by the Executive in the context of military action, it would turn our system of checks and balances on its head to suggest that a citizen could not make his way to court with a challenge to the factual basis for his detention by his government, simply because the Executive opposes making available such a challenge.

Justice David Souter went even further in his concurring opinion. Citing the "cautionary example of the internments [of Japanese-Americans] in World War II," he noted that experience suggests that the "defining character of American constitutional government is its constant tension between security and liberty, serving both by partial helpings of each." Then, citing "inescapable human nature," Souter emphasized the need to check the actions of the executive—the branch of the government primarily responsible for countering the threat to our security. He reminded us of Justice Robert Jackson's observation that "the president is not commander in chief of the country, only of the military," and that the other branches of government must play an important role in striking the proper balance between security and liberty.

Perhaps the most interesting opinion was a dissent written by Justice Antonin Scalia, who is the personification of the "dead-constitution" school of interpretation. In an earlier chapter of this book, written before the June 2004 decisions were rendered, I speculated about whether a "dead constitution," whose interpretation does not change with the times, might prove more protective of individual rights during times of crisis than a "living constitution," whose interpretation can both expand and contract rights depending on the circumstances.[4] In the *Hamdi* case, Justice Scalia provided some support for this speculation. He went much further than the majority in his interpretation of the constitutional rights of American citizens detained during an emergency. Citing the original understanding of the Constitution, especially its inclusion of the historic writ of habeas corpus, Scalia argued that the government could not continue to detain Hamdi simply by declaring his confinement to be non-criminal and nonpunitive:

> It is unthinkable that the Executive could render otherwise criminal grounds for detention non-criminal merely by disclaiming an intent to prosecute, or by asserting that it was incapacitating dangerous offenders rather than punishing wrongdoing. . . . ("A finding of dangerousness standing alone, is ordinarily not a sufficient ground upon which to justify indefinite involuntary commitment.")
>
> These due process rights have historically been vindicated by the writ of habeas corpus. . . . The writ of habeas corpus was preserved in

the constitution—the only common-law writ to be explicitly mentioned. See Art. I, 9, cl. 2. Hamilton lauded "the establishment of the writ of *habeas corpus*" in his Federalist defense as a means to protect against "the practice of arbitrary imprisonments . . . in all ages, [one of] the favourite and most formidable instruments of tyranny." The Federalist No. 84, *supra,* at 444. Indeed, availability of the writ under the new Constitution (along with the requirement of trial by jury in criminal cases, see Art. III, 2, cl. 3) was his basis for arguing that additional, explicit procedural protections were unnecessary.

Scalia would have ordered Hamdi's immediate release unless he were to be charged as a criminal and provided with the rights accorded criminal defendants—or unless Congress decided to suspend the writ of habeas corpus.* Scalia accused the majority of interpreting our old constitution "as though writing a new constitution . . . with an unheard-of system in which the citizen rather than the government bears the burden of proof, testimony is by hearsay rather than live witnesses, and the presiding officer may well be a 'neutral' military officer rather than a judge or a jury." He accused the plurality of

what might be called a Mr. Fix-it Mentality. The plurality seems to view it as its mission to Make Everything Come Out Right, rather than merely to decree the consequences, as far as individual rights are concerned, of the other two branches' actions and omissions. Has the Legislature failed to suspend the writ in the current dire emergency? Well, we will remedy that failure by prescribing the reasonable conditions

---

*Scalia seems to believe, erroneously in my view, that a congressional decision to suspend the writ is not subject to judicial review: "But whether the attacks of September 11, 2001 constitute an 'invasion,' and whether those attacks still justify suspension several years later, are questions for Congress *rather than this Court*" (emphasis added). Whether Scalia means *initially* for Congress or *ultimately* for Congress is unclear. Were Congress to suspend the writ unlawfully—for example, during peacetime—surely the courts should give no effect to such a blatantly unconstitutional suspension.

that a suspension should have included. And has the Executive failed to live up to those reasonable conditions? Well, we will ourselves make that failure good, so that this dangerous fellow (if he is dangerous) need not be set free. The problem with this approach is not only that it steps out of the courts' modest and limited role in a democratic society; but that by repeatedly doing what it thinks the political branches ought to do it encourages their lassitude and saps the vitality of government by the people.

This "Mr. Fix-it Mentality" is—according to Scalia—an inevitable outgrowth of the "living constitution" school. That school may interpret constitutional rights broadly during relatively tranquil times, but it tends to contract rights during difficult times, as he believes it did in this case. Under Scalia's "dead constitution" approach, the Constitution would remain the same during good and bad times, with rights neither expanding nor contracting. Indeed Scalia believes that the founders intended constitutional rights to be fully applicable precisely during times of national crisis:

> The Founders warned us about the risk [of curtailing rights during emergencies] and equipped us with a Constitution designed to deal with it.
>
> Many think it not only inevitable but entirely proper that liberty give way to security in times of national crisis—that, at the extremes of military exigency, *inter arma silent leges*. Whatever the general merits of the view that war silences law or modulates its voice, that view has no place in the interpretation and application of a Constitution designed precisely to confront war and, in a manner that accords with democratic principles, to accommodate it.[5]

This debate over the nature of constitutional interpretation raises deeper questions about the nature of experiential rights.

*Does the Experiential Theory of Rights, Like the
"Living Constitution" School of Interpretation,
Lead to the Occasional Contraction of Rights,
As Well As to Their Expansion?*

The debate between those, like Justice Scalia, who advocate a "dead constitution" and those, like Justice O'Connor, who seem to favor a more living constitution, transcends the current terrorist threat. It has deep implications for any theory of rights in a democracy. I end this book, therefore, with a discussion of how an experiential approach to rights, though generally expansive of most individual rights, may sometimes justify their contraction.

From the earliest days of our constitutional history, a debate has raged about how to interpret the open-ended words of our charter of government. Should these words, written years earlier, be constantly reinterpreted to address "current problems and current needs"? Or should they mean precisely what those who wrote them intended them to mean? The "reinterpretation" school is best represented by the judicial opinions and writings of Justice William J. Brennan, who served on the Supreme Court from 1956 to 1990, and by my colleague and friend Laurence Tribe, the distinguished constitutional law professor and litigator. The "original understanding" approach is best represented by current Supreme Court Justice Antonin Scalia, who joined the high court in 1986.

Both sides to the debate begin by agreeing with the broad principles enunciated by Chief Justice John Marshall in 1803, that "it is a constitution we are expounding"*—a constitution that was "designed to approach immortality as nearly as any human institution can approach it." The disagreement is about whether the "reinter-

---

*One of my very liberal professors at law school used to engage in a takeoff on Marshall's words and say, "It's a constitution we are *expanding*," to which one of my more conservative professors would respond, "No, it is a constitution we are *expunging*."

pretation" approach or the "original meaning" approach is more likely to assure immortality.

Those who advocate the "reinterpretation" approach argue that in order to assure that words written more than two centuries ago remain relevant today, they should be interpreted in light of changing experiences. According to this view, the framers of our Constitution purposely used "broad and majestic terms"—such as "equal protection of the laws," "due process," "cruel and unusual punishment," and "liberty"—which were "left to gather meaning from experience." They recognized that "only a stagnant society remains unchanged,"[6] and that "the genius of our constitution is not in any static meaning it might have in a world that is dead and gone, but the adaptability of the great principles to cope with current problems and current needs."[7] Thus, to remain faithful to the real meaning of the Constitution, its broad phrases must be reinterpreted as times change, in order to implement "the substantive value choices" of the framers and apply them to new circumstances that these men could not have contemplated when they wrote the Constitution.* By reinterpreting the Constitution to make it relevant to changing conditions, the judges bring it alive. It becomes a living document.

This "living constitution" school of interpretation is opposed by those who argue that the original meaning of the document's words must always govern. If this original meaning does not suit modern times, then the Constitution should be changed by the popular branches of government through the amending process. It should not be changed by the elite judiciary whose job it is to apply the existing law rather than to bring it up to date or "fix it" by repeated reinterpretation.

---

*This sort of interpretation is only applicable to the kinds of broad phrases mentioned above. No matter how much circumstances may have changed since 1787, the constitutional requirement that a president must be 35 years old cannot be reinterpreted, since there is no textual ambiguity about "35 years old."

The most vocal proponent of this school has been Justice Scalia, who has provocatively characterized the U.S. Constitution as a "dead" document. He rejects, as "the conventional fallacy," the idea that the Constitution is a "living document"—that is, a text whose meaning may differ from generation to generation with changing experiences. Instead he believes the Constitution means precisely "what it meant when it was adopted." Scalia argues that such a mode of interpretation makes the Constitution more "enduring."[8]

This debate has deep roots in the intellectual history of Western civilization and goes back at least to Talmudic times. A legend is told in the Talmud about an argument between a rabbi who believed in a "dead" Bible and a group of rabbis who believed in a "living" Bible. The focus of the argument was an arcane law about an oven. To support his interpretation of the law, Rabbi Eliezer invoked the original intent of the author of the Torah, God himself. Eliezer implored, "If the halachah [the authoritative meaning of the law] agrees with me, let it be proved from heaven!"—whereupon a heavenly voice cried out to the others: "Why do ye dispute with R[abbi] Eliezer, seeing that . . . the halachah agrees with him!" (Pretty authoritative evidence of the original intent!) But another rabbi rose up and rebuked God for interfering in this very human dispute. "Thou hast long since written the Torah" and "we pay no attention to a Heavenly Voice." The message was clear: God's children were telling their father, "It is our job, as the rabbis, to give meaning to the Torah that you gave us. You gave us a document to interpret, and a methodology for interpreting it. Now leave us to do our job." God agreed, laughing with joy, "My . . . [children] have defeated me in argument."[9]

No single person—divine or otherwise—drafted the American Constitution, its Bill of Rights, or its post–Civil War amendments (which together comprise our current Constitution). Indeed, the Constitution is full of mistakes, poor choice of language, and other manifestations of the obvious haste in which it was written. Our contemporary rabbis in robes cannot call for a heavenly—or even an earthly—voice to confirm the correctness of their constructions of such terms as *due process, equal protection, freedom of speech,* or *cruel and unusual punishment.* But I wonder if Jefferson, Madison, Hamilton—and our other farsighted framers—would not respond to a contemporary Eliezer's call for authoritative interpretation by declining to interfere and by saying: "It is a Constitution you must expound. We wrote its phrases long ago in a different era. Pay no attention to those who invoke voices of certainty from the grave or the heavens."

But to ignore completely the intent of the framers would be as simpleminded and meaningless as pretending to know with certainty the precise and singular meaning of language that was probably selected, at least in part, for its open-endedness and its capacity for redefinition over time.

In recent decades, this debate over the proper mode of constitutional interpretation has taken on a distinctively ideological tone. Liberals, such as Justices William Brennan, Arthur Goldberg, Earl Warren, and Ruth Bader Ginsburg have argued in favor of a "living" constitution whose rights are capable of being "*expanded* beyond its original narrow purview."[10] Justice Ginsburg has observed that an important part of our history "is the story of the *extension* of constitutional rights and protections to people once ignored or excluded."[11] Professor Tribe insists that our living constitution "invites us, and our judges, to *expand on* the . . . freedoms that are uniquely part of our heritage."[12] These liberals see the Constitution as "evolving"—that is, moving toward *more* liberty, *more* equality, and *more* due process. They fear that the opposite trend will move us backward toward a "stagnant, archaic, hidebound document steeped in the prejudices and superstitions of a time long past."[13] Nor do they agree with those who claim that a "dead constitution" will "depoliticize" or limit the power of the judiciary in an ideologically neutral manner. They argue instead that:

The political underpinnings of such a choice should not escape notice. A position that upholds constitutional claims only if they were within the specific contemplation of the framers in effect establishes a presumption of resolving textual ambiguities against the claim of constitutional right. It is far from clear what justifies such a presumption against claims of right. Nothing intrinsic in the nature of interpretation—if there is such a thing as the "nature" of interpretation—commands such a passive approach to ambiguity. This is a choice no less political than any other; it expresses antipathy to claims of the minority rights against the majority. Those who would restrict claims of right to the values of 1789 specifically articulated in the Constitution turn a blind eye to social process and eschew adaptation of overarching principles and changes of social circumstance.[14]

In other words, the liberals acknowledge that their preferred mode of interpreting their "living constitution" serves to *expand* rights, because they see the Constitution as an "evolving" document that moves in one direction. According to at least some of them, it is a ratchet that locks movement only in the forward position—toward more liberty, equality, due process, etc. They insist, however, that the conservatives' preferred mode of interpreting their "dead constitution" serves to *contract* rights by limiting them to "the standards that prevailed in 1685 when Lord Jeffreys presided over the Bloody Assizes or when the Bill of Rights was adopted." According to this view, the conservative approach is anything but neutral. It reflects old-fashioned views of limited rights that just happen to correspond largely with the ideological preferences of those who feel bound by the original understanding of the Constitution.

The liberals are generally correct as a descriptive matter. Most contemporary justices and scholars who advocate a living constitution are, in fact, liberals whose personal perspectives favor an expansive, evolving approach to constitutional rights. And most of those who advocate a dead constitution are, in fact, conservatives whose personal predispositions favor a narrowing of constitutional rights.[15]

There is, however, a third approach beyond the "liberal-living-evolving" constitution, on the one hand, and the "conservative-dead-original meaning" constitution, on the other hand. A living constitution that is capable of adapting to changing circumstances need not always move only in one direction. It need not always "expand" or "evolve." A capacity to adapt to changing circumstances may also entail, on occasion, some contraction, some moving backward, some de-volution.

Although Justice Brennan always tried to push his living constitution in one direction only, he seemed to recognize that backward movement is possible as well. He wrote that "each generation has the choice to overrule or add to the fundamental principles enumerated by the framers." He recognized that the Constitution must adapt to "good or bad tendencies of which no prophecy can be made."[16]

Justice Scalia too seems to have recognized the two-way nature of the living constitution even before the recent terrorism cases: "One may reasonably ask—once the original import of the Constitution is cast aside to be replaced by the 'fundamental values' of the current society—why are we invited only to 'expand on' freedoms, and not to contract them as well?"[17] He observes that "the record of history refutes the proposition that the evolving Constitution will invariably enlarge individual rights."[18] (The Talmudic victory for the living Torah school of interpretation has resulted in both expansion and contraction of biblical prescriptions.)[19]

In our current age of terrorism, when weapons of mass destruction are capable of destroying so much so quickly, we may have to reevaluate the scope of certain rights and the trend toward their expansion. Consider, for example, the right to anonymity, which the Supreme

Court has recognized in several important contexts, especially where disclosure of one's identity might chill the exercise of speech, press, or assembly rights. Surely today, no one could reasonably argue that an individual's right to anonymity should deny the government the power to demand proper identification from anyone seeking to board an airplane. Nor would this power be limited only to "optional" means of travel, such as airplanes. There is little doubt that the government may properly demand identification from anyone seeking to enter a governmental building, including a courthouse or a legislative chamber in which there is a right to petition government for a redress of grievances. Proper identification may also be required of train, bus, and ship travelers—as well as car drivers, taxpayers, social security recipients, and many others. If Congress were to impose a national identification system on all adults, I believe it would be upheld today, though I would not have been as certain forty years ago. The threat of terrorism has altered the balance between the right of anonymity and the need for security. Experience is pressuring us to contract the former as we expand the latter.

Thus, at the same time as experience is pushing us in the direction of expanding certain privacy rights—most notably the right to engage in private homosexual conduct without governmental intervention—other aspects of that same right are being contracted.

The same can be said about the right against self-incrimination. The Supreme Court reaffirmed the *Miranda* rule in the context of traditional police interrogation designed to elicit incriminating admissions about past crimes, while at the same time giving a green light to government officials to elicit intelligence information deemed necessary to prevent future terrorist attacks.

We are likely to see more of this in the future as the courts look to the new experiences with terrorism to interpret our living constitution in ways that contract some rights, expand others, while leaving some essentially unchanged. This is the nature of a living, breathing constitution adapting to both "good and bad tendencies." This is the true "genius of the constitution," resting not on any static meaning it might have had in a world before the threats of mass-destruction terrorism—"a world that is dead and gone"—but in the "adaptability of the great principles to cope with current problems and current needs," such as those caused by terrorism.

The shoes are now on other feet. Those who advocate a living constitution must be prepared to consider some contraction of those rights that may be incompatible with our current need to prevent terrorism. Those who claim that a "dead constitution" assures that rights will remain unchanged regardless of pressing social needs must now resist any contraction of our rights, at least as their scope was understood by our founding fathers.

It will be interesting to see whether neutral principles of interpretation trump ideological result orientation. If they do, then Justice Scalia may emerge as the "liberal" during this age of terrorism, insisting that the courts not cut back on any rights contained in our dead constitution. Those who advocate a living constitution may, on the other hand, assume the role of conservatives, cutting back on established rights in an effort to adapt the Constitution to new wrongs.[20]

Experience shows, however, that few if any justices will always remain true to their articulated principles of judicial interpretation. Justice Scalia openly violated his own espoused principles when he believed that a presidential election might be at stake.[21] He became "Mr. Fix-it" in *Bush v. Gore,* effectively voting to assure the victory of a politically conservative administration, while justices who advocate a living constitution have often become hide-bound traditionalists when new wrongs pose challenges to old rights.[22]

Experience also shows that justices do not always have the final word on rights. Though their role has not proved to be as "modest and limited" in our democratic society as Scalia wishes it were, it is constrained by the power of the executive and legislative branches, and ultimately by the people. Our system of checks and balances operates to limit the courts, as well as the legislature and the president. Consider, for example, another potentially explosive case that came before the high court in the 2003–2004 term. That case, *Elk Grove Unified School District v. Michael A. Newdow,* raised the question of whether Congress's decision in 1954 to add the words "under God" to our pledge of allegiance violated the First Amendment's requirement that Congress "make no law respecting an establishment of religion." Despite its role as the final arbiter of constitutionality, the Supreme Court simply lacked the political power to strike those two words from the pledge.[23] Had the justices ruled that the inclusion of these words violated the Constitution, the political reaction would have been immediate: The Constitution would have been amended to overrule the decision. The justices understood this reality and devised a way to avoid deciding the case on the merits, ruling instead that the atheist father who brought the lawsuit did not have legal standing to speak on behalf of his ten-year-old daughter, over whom he did not have custody.

In the end, the people rule in a democracy. No judicial decision will long survive if it contradicts the felt experiences of the citizens. This is why those of us who believe that a rights-based democracy, and certain rights in particular, are essential to our future must not limit our advocacy to the courts. We must take our case for rights to the people.[24] We must constantly prove that rights work, that they are necessary to prevent wrongs, and that they are worth the price we sometimes pay for them. Because human beings and their governments will always come up with new ways of inflicting grievous wrongs on other human beings, we must constantly construct new rights. Because rights are a process for achieving liberty and fairness rather than an end in themselves, the struggle for rights never stays won. Because there will always be wrongs, there must always be rights.

NOTES

Introduction

1. The title of this chapter deliberately violates the "Preposition Prescription." I defer to the Virginia English Bulletin for my grammatical defense: "The Preposition Prescription, one of the more infamous 'rules' of English grammar, traces its genesis . . . to Robert Lowth [author of *A Short Introduction to English Grammar*, published in 1762], who argued that because Latin sentences did not end in prepositions, English sentences should not either." But Lowth also wrote that it "is an idiom, which our language is strongly inclined to: it prevails in common conversation, and suits very well with the familiar style in writing" (quote from Bryan A. Garner, *A Dictionary of Modern American Usage*, New York: Oxford University Press, 1998). The Bulletin continues: "The rule has been attacked by countless writers and linguists, but it has proved unusually robust. . . . Perhaps the most famous remark is that attributed to Winston Churchill, who reportedly objected that 'this is the sort of arrant pedantry up with which I will not put!'" (See http://www.people.virginia.edu/~hl5s/fumbled.html.) Another wag solemnly declared that "a preposition is a word not to end a sentence with."

2. Quoted in Ron Chernow, *Alexander Hamilton* (New York: Penguin, 2004), p. 60.

3. Alessandra Stanley, "Understanding the President and His God," *New York Times*, April 29, 2004, p. E1.

4. See David McGowan, "Ethos in Law and History: Alexander Hamilton, *The Federalist*, and the Supreme Court," 85 *Minnesota Law Review* 755 (2001), pp. 778–779 (noting Hamilton's support, as demonstrated by his reaction to the Virginia and Kentucky resolutions, which opposed the Alien and Sedition Acts; among other things, Hamilton recommended using military force to "persuade" Virginia that the Alien and Sedition Acts were appropriate).

5. John Hart Ely put it this way: "Technically, of course, reason alone can't tell you anything: it can only connect premises to conclusions." Ely, *Democracy and Distrust: A Theory of Judicial Review* (Cambridge, Mass.: Harvard University Press, 1980), p. 56. I would add that it can help structure a process by which we derive rights from experience.

6. See Robert Reich, "The Last Word," *The American Prospect*, July 1, 2004.

7. We have officially apologized for this disgraceful action and paid reparations, despite the Supreme Court's having approved it as constitutional.

8. Justice Scalia has remained true to this approach in certain cases; see, e.g., *Maryland v. Craig*, 497 U.S. 836 (1990) (dissenting opinion) and *Hamdi v. Rumsfeld*, 542 U.S. _____ (2004). In other cases, however, he has voted to contract rights, despite his rhetoric of consistency over time. In virtually no cases has he voted to expand rights, except when such an expansion served his political and ideological agenda. See, e.g., *Bush v. Gore*, 531 U.S. 98 (2000). See also the Conclusion, *infra*.

Chapter 1

1. *Right* also means "correct." I use it here in its other meaning: a claim that can be asserted by an individual against the power of government.

2. Under a positivist approach, one claim of right may prevail over another, but only if the power to trump also derives from humanly enacted legal authority. For example, a federal constitutional right generally supersedes a state constitutional right, because the federal constitution—which was ratified by the states—contains a supremacy clause that grants superior authority to properly exercised federal constitutional rights. In theory, positive law may derive from a God-given legal document such as the Bible. But the term, as generally used, does not include divine positive law.

3. *Lochner v. New York*, 198 U.S. 45 (1905), at p. 75, dissenting opinion.

4. See Albert W. Alschuler, *Law Without Values: The Life, Work, and Legacy of Justice Holmes* (Chicago: University of Chicago Press, 2000).

5. Lloyd Weinreb, *Natural Law and Justice* (Cambridge, Mass.: Harvard University Press, 1987), p. 99. This formulation obviously oversimplifies an enormously complex body of thinking, but in broad outlines is accurate.

6. *Boston Globe*, August 25, 2000, p. A23.

Chapter 2

1. H. L. A. Hart, *Essays in Jurisprudence and Philosophy* (New York: Oxford University Press, 1983), p. 163.

2. These comments were first reported in the Israeli newspaper *Haaretz* on June 25, 2003. Former Palestinian Authority Prime Minister Abu Mazen said in a meeting with militants that Bush had made the statements in an earlier meeting in Aqaba. Al Kamen wrote in the *Washington Post* on June 27, 2003, that calls to the White House for clarification on the comments "went unreturned," but that there is a possibility the quotes were muddled somewhere along the line. "After all," Kamen wrote, "this is Abu Mazen's account in Arabic of what Bush said in English, written down by a notetaker in Arabic, then back into English."

3. Interview with *Time*, January 11, 1999.

4. Fatwa issued February 1998.

5. See *The 9/11 Commission Report: Final Report of the National Commission on Terrorist Attacks Upon the United States* (New York: W.W. Norton, 2004), at p. 380. See also Marc Lacey, "In Sudan, Hunter and Hunted Alike Invoke the Prophet," *New York Times*, August 22, 2004, p. 3. See also Michael Ignatieff, *The Lesser Evil: Political Ethics in an Age of Terror* (Princeton, N.J.: Princeton University Press, 2004), p. 124 for a quotation from Osama bin Laden justifying, in the name of Allah, the killing of Muslims who betray "their own prophet."

6. Though I am not an advocate of divine law, a case can be made that Jewish tradition (or at least some renderings of it) supports a human, process-based positive law rather than an externally based natural law. The Bible commands that "justice shall you pursue," suggesting that the quest for justice is an active continuing process. Then there is the wonderful story of the rabbis who reject God's own voice as the authoritative source of law and instead look to the process of legal decision-making established by the Halakah. See the Conclusion, *infra* at p. 226. The human process—from the Mishnah to the Gemorah to the responsa—continues to this day. In reality, it is far more akin to the common-law process of legal development than to the divine-law process of discovering "revealed" law, though it purports to partake of the latter as well.

7. Lieberman was quoting George Washington, who was not a particularly religious person, especially in terms of organized churches. Richard Perez-Pena, "Lieberman Seeks Greater Role for Religion in Public Life," *New York Times,* August 28, 2000, p. A1.

8. See Alan Dershowitz, "Keyes' campaign twists founding fathers' words," *Baltimore Sun*, August 15, 2004, p. C5.

9. See Alan Dershowitz, *America Declares Independence* (Hoboken, N.J.: Wiley, 2003), pp. 1–84.

Chapter 3

1. Blaise Pascal, *Les Pensees,* XXIV (1670); Dante, *De Monarchia* (c. 1313).

2. John R. Searle, *Speech Acts: An Essay in the Philosophy of Language* (Cambridge: Cambridge University Press, 1977), p. 132. See, generally, George Edward Moore, *Principia Ethica* (Cambridge: Cambridge University Press, 1960).

3. Juvenal, *Satires* XIV (A.D. 128); Saint Augustine, *Of Conscience* (c. 425); John Florio, *His Firste Fruites* (1578); Cicero, *De senectute* XIX (c. 78 B.C.). The word "nature" has many meanings, especially when translated from several languages. The quotations here are intended merely as illustrative of a range of views on the subject.

4. David's son Solomon came closer to the truth when he observed in Ecclesiastes that he had seen "a just man that perisheth in his righteousness, and . . . a wicked man that prolongeth his life in his wickedness." Eccles. 7:15.

5. Baruch Spinoza, *Ethica I* (1677). Pope's poem was printed in the memorial program at the service for Steve Gould because it had been set to music and sung by Steve's choral group. When it came my turn to speak, I felt compelled to note that my politically radical friend would hardly have accepted its conclusion in the sphere of politics.

6. Robert G. Ingersoll, "Some Reasons Why," 1881; from *The Works of Robert G. Ingersoll*, vol. II (New York: The Ingersoll League, 1929), p. 315.

7. Pierre Bayle, *Pensees diverses sur la comete* (1680).

8. See T. W. Adorno, *The Authoritarian Personality* (New York: Harper, 1950).

9. Frederick Kidder, *History of the Boston Massacre, March 5, 1770* (Albany, 1870). Reprinted by the Notable Trials Library (New York: Pantheon, 2001).

10. Oliver Wendell Holmes Jr., in *The Common Law* (Boston: Little, Brown and Co., 1881).

11. Very rudimentarily, according to John Rawls's *A Theory of Justice* (Cambridge, Mass.: Belknap Press, 1999), the "original position" is a hypothetical situation in which rational, risk-averse, calculating individuals choose principles of social relations under which they would do best. These individuals, however, are placed behind the "veil of ignorance"—essentially a location where they do not know their age, sex, religious belief, or any other information that might be particular to them, but should be irrelevant to principles of justice.

12. Immanuel Kant, *Metaphysische Anfangsgründe der Rechtslehre,* quoted in Rawls, *A Theory of Justice,* p. 128.

Chapter 4

1. From Justice Jackson's concurring opinion in *Krulewitch v. United States,* 336 U.S. 440 (1949), at p. 458. Charles-Louis de Secondat, Baron de Montesquieu, made a similar observation in 1742: "There is no crueler tyranny than that which is perpetrated under the shield of law and in the name of justice."

2. Ronald Dworkin, *Taking Rights Seriously* (Cambridge, Mass.: Harvard University Press, 1977), pp. 177, xi, 184.

3. Ibid., p. 198.

4. Ibid., p. 176.

5. Ibid., p. xi.

6. See Mary Ann Glendon, *Rights Talk: The Impoverishment of Political Discourse* (New York: Free Press, 1993).

7. Dworkin, *Taking Rights Seriously,* p. 272.

8. Jean Piaget, a highly influential thinker in the field of the psychology of child development, found that children start in a "heteronomous" moral reasoning phase, marked by obedience to authority and rigid observation of rules. This stage eventually gives way to an autonomous stage, in which children examine rules critically and apply them in order to achieve a new goal of cooperation and mutual respect. A child, he found, formulates his or her morality by working to arrive at fair solutions to problems. See, generally, Jean Piaget, *The Moral Judgment of the Child* (New York: Free Press, 1997). Lawrence Kohlberg built upon Piaget's work. He identified six stages of moral development, progress through which was spurred by social interaction, and he held that moral education should focus on helping individuals mature to the next stage, rather than emphasizing traditional values. Kohlberg believed that

certain principles of justice and fairness served as the pinnacle of the development of one's morality, since they are found in a wide range of cultures worldwide. See, generally, Lawrence Kohlberg, *Essays on Moral Development*, 2 vols. (New York: Harper, 1981 and 1984).

9. Harvard psychology professor Marc Hauser found that "monkeys employ rule-like strategies for promoting the welfare of a group, including maintaining peace, observing boundaries, and sharing food. And they can abide by these rules without necessarily understanding them. Humans are a different kind of animal: We can consciously evaluate whether behavior is right or wrong, but we tend to do so depending on the conventions of our society." Marc Hauser, "Morals, Apes, and Us," *Discover,* February 2000. What people say about the rights of others, and how they act when these rights conflict with their own preferences, are somewhat different matters.

10. Dworkin, *Taking Rights Seriously*, p. 81.

11. Ibid., p. 160.

12. Ibid.

13. The debate over equality of outcome versus equality of opportunity is a long-standing one. One such exchange featuring several prominent thinkers was published in the *Boston Review,* vol. 20, April/May 1995.

14. Dworkin, *Taking Rights Seriously*, p. 177.

15. Ibid., p. 271.

16. See generally Michael J. Sandel, *Democracy's Discontent: America in Search of a Public Philosophy* (Cambridge, Mass.: Harvard University Press, 1996).

17. In fairness to Dworkin, I have been unable to find a single place where he presents a comprehensive theory of the origin of rights. My criticism is based largely on selective quotations, in a variety of contexts, from his masterful book *Taking Rights Seriously.*

Chapter 5

1. Ronald Dworkin, *Taking Rights Seriously* (Cambridge, Mass.: Harvard University Press, 1977), p. 190. See also Alan Dershowitz, *America Declares Independence* (Hoboken, N.J.: Wiley, 2003).

2. See dissenting opinion of Justice Breyer in *Hiibel v. Sixth Judicial District Court of Nevada*, 542 U.S. _____ (2004).

3. The defendant also claimed a Fifth Amendment right against self-incrimination, but the court concluded that it "need not resolve" Fifth Amendment issues in this case because there was little likelihood that providing his name would incriminate this defendant in this context.

4. See *Hamdi v. Rumsfeld*, 542 U.S. _____ (2004).

5. See William Glaberson, "Word for Word/The Second Amendment Debate; To Bear or Not to Bear: It Depends on How You Read History," in "Week in Review," *New York Times,* September 24, 2000, p. 7.

6. Dan Eggen, "FBI Curbed in Tracking Gun Buyers," *Washington Post,* November 18, 2003, p. A1.

7. Kristin Luker, *Abortion and the Politics of Motherhood* (Berkeley: University of California Press, 1984).

8. Paul Robinson, writing in the *New York Times Book Review,* May 6, 1984.

9. See *Lawrence v. Texas,* 539 U.S. 558 (2003). In August 2004, Zanzibar enacted a law punishing adult consensual homosexual sex by 25 years in prison.

10. John Hart Ely, *Democracy and Distrust* (Cambridge, Mass.: Harvard University Press, 1980), p. 50.

11. Ibid.

Chapter 6

1. H. L. A. Hart, *Essays in Jurisprudence and Philosophy* (New York: Oxford University Press, 1983), p. 196.

2. Ibid., p. 198.

3. Thomas Jefferson felt that "without fear of punishment beyond the grave, individuals lacked an incentive to behave well and that, without hope of reuniting with loved ones, family commitments and friendships would lose their gravity." See the Jewish Virtual Library (http://www.jewishvirtuallibrary.org/jsource) and also Dershowitz, *America Declares Independence* (Hoboken, N.J.: Wiley, 2003).

4. Hart, *Essays,* p. 198.

5. Fyodor Dostoyevsky, *The Brothers Karamazov* (New York: Modern Library, 1996), p. 282.

6. There are, of course, many variations on these three sources, including intuition, logic, and inspiration.

7. Of course the Native Americans had discovered, and lived along, the Mississippi before de Soto.

Chapter 7

1. See Bill for Establishing Religious Freedom, Section I, online at http://teachingamericanhistory.org/library/index.asp?document=23 (accessed August 25, 2004).

2. Alvin H. Rosenfeld and Irving Greenberg, *Confronting the Holocaust: The Impact of Elie Wiesel* (Bloomington: Indiana University Press, 1979).

3. But see Albert W. Alschuler, *Law Without Values: The Life, Work, and Legacy of Justice Holmes* (Chicago: University of Chicago Press, 2000).

4. An interesting postwar prosecution in Germany illustrates the dilemma of dealing with positive law that is later deemed immoral. Toward the end of the Nazi regime a woman who wanted to be rid of her husband turned him in to the Gestapo for insulting Hitler. The husband was punished under the law. After the war was over

the wife was prosecuted for illegally depriving her husband of his liberty. She defended herself by pointing to the fact that her husband's deprivation of liberty was pursuant to German positive law and thus could not be deemed criminal. The appellate court affirmed the wife's conviction, ruling that the statute under which her husband was punished was "contrary to the sound conscience and sense of justice of all decent human beings." This reliance on natural law to trump positive law was clearly a reaction to Nazi positivism, which declared *Gesetz als Gesetz* (law is law) and demanded compliance with the most immoral of laws. Legal philosophers who were positivists before the war became proponents of natural law after experiencing the legal abuses of Nazism.

5. William Nicholls, *Christian Antisemitism: A History of Hate* (Northvale, N.J.: Jason Aronson, 1993), p. 360. Nicholls goes on:

> The conflicts in question would have been, one presumes, between their duty to God and their duty to the Nazi state. Perhaps, too, he had in mind the casuistic argument that if he did not formally condemn actions against the Jews, Germans who took part could be said to have sinned in ignorance, thus incurring a lesser spiritual penalty.
>
> This is false compassion, apart from its implications for Pius's view of the moral priorities between saving Jews and the mental comfort of his own flock. Moreover, the argument is hardly convincing. Even given the anti-Jewish conditioning we have been describing, no one with a Catholic education could have been wholly in ignorance of the fact that actually killing defenseless Jews, or even taking part in measures leading to that end, was a mortal sin, whatever their duty to state, and whether or not the pope chose to say so. But this does not remove the pope's responsibility to warn and condemn.
>
> On his own premises, the pope must have imperilled the eternal salvation of German and East European Catholics far more by his silence than he could have done by speaking, since he failed to direct them away from actions objectively evil beyond measure. Without the moral support of his outspoken condemnation, hundreds of thousands of Catholics gave in and took part in the most evil act of all history, unrebuked by their spiritual leader.

Pp. 360–361. See also David Kertzner, *The Vatican's Role in the Rise of Anti-Semitism* (New York: Knopf, 2001).

6. See the *New York Times,* November 2, 2000, p. A6.

7. Mary Ann Glendon, *A World Made New: Eleanor Roosevelt and the Universal Declaration of Human Rights* (New York: Random House, 2001).

8. Marlise Simons, "Tribunal in the Hague Finds Bosnian Serb Guilty of Genocide," *New York Times,* August 3, 2001; Reuters, "Three Bosnian Muslim Officers Face War Crimes in the Hague," *New York Times,* August 4, 2001.

9. In Judaism, it is believed that humanity was created with two competing impulses—*yetzer tov* (a good impulse) and *yetzer ra* (an evil impulse). The *yetzer tov*

serves as people's moral conscience, while the *yetzer ra* drives people to satisfy their personal needs and desires. The *yetzer ra* is not intrinsically bad; it becomes bad when it is not countervailed by *yetzer tov* and leads to wrongdoing. See Genesis 6:5, 8:21; Berachos 61a; Sukkah 52a.

10. Stephen Jay Gould, *Wonderful Life: The Burgess Shale and the Nature of History* (New York: Norton, 1989).

11. Quoted in Richard P. Feynman, *What Do YOU Care What Other People Think?* (New York: Norton, 1988), p. 241.

Chapter 8

1. They were overt about their desire to rid Europe of Jews, but once they decided on genocide, rather than expulsion, they went to great lengths to disguise the death camps as work camps and to use euphemisms such as "deportation to the East." See Robert Rozett and Shmuel Spector, *Encyclopedia of the Holocaust* (New York: Facts on File, 2000), pp. 187–189, and Jack R. Fischel, *Historical Dictionary of the Holocaust* (Lanham, Md.: Scarecrow, 1999).

2. "The Politics of Aristotle," quoted in Michael J. Sandel, *Liberalism and the Limits of Justice,* 2nd ed. (Cambridge: Cambridge University Press, 1998), p. xi.

3. Meditation III.

4. See Richard P. Feynman, *What Do YOU Care What Other People Think?* (New York: Norton, 1988), p. 29.

5. But see Justice Antonin Scalia in *Troxel v. Granville,* 530 U.S. 57 (2000), at p. 91.

6. John Hart Ely, *Democracy and Distrust* (Cambridge, Mass.: Harvard University Press, 1980), p. 49. Even the ancients recognized the potential for abuse and misuse of natural law in advocacy.

7. Ibid.

8. Feynman, *What Do YOU Care What Other People Think?*, p. 245.

9. Ibid., p. 248.

10. Thomas Hobbes, *Leviathan* (1651), Chapter 18.

11. Stephen Jay Gould and Niles Eldredge, "Punctuated Equilibria: The Tempo and Mode of Evolution Reconsidered," *Paleobiology* 3 (1977), pp. 115–151. See also "Punctuated Equilibrium" by Francis Heylighen at Principia Cybernetica Web (http://pespmc1.vub.ac.be/Punctueq.html; accessed August 25, 2004). The Gould–Eldredge Theory was not without its critics, one of whom, unfairly but cleverly, called it "evolution by jerks."

12. See Mary Ann Glendon, "Foundations of Human Rights: The Unfinished Business," *American Journal of Jurisprudence,* 44 (1999), p. 1. See also Jacques Maritain, *The Rights of Man and Natural Law* (San Francisco: Ignatius Press, 1986), pp. 126–127. There was also a burgeoning of certain human rights following the 30 million casualties of World War I.

13. Fifteen years after the Chinese government killed hundreds of unarmed pro-democracy protestors in Tiananmen Square in an act that drew international condemnation, Amnesty International reports that it believes people are still imprisoned

for their part in the protests, and that the government continues to detain people who have attempted to commemorate the killings.

14. After the Warren Court rendered its decisions that applied several provisions of the Bill of Rights to the states and provided safeguards for criminal defendants, it was widely believed that the court had facilitated a crime wave. This created a public backlash in favor of law and order that helped Richard Nixon win election to the White House in 1968. See, generally, Corinna Barrett Lain, "Countermajoritarian Hero or Zero? Rethinking the Warren Court's Role in the Criminal Procedure Revolution," *University of Pennsylvania Law Review*, 152 (2004), pp. 1361–1452.

15. Up until now, most of the contractions of rights have been limited to noncitizens, especially Muslims and Arabs.

16. Among the individuals responsible for the detention of 100,000 Japanese Americans were liberals such as Franklin Delano Roosevelt, Abe Fortas, and Earl Warren.

17. In 1971, Congress did repeal the Emergency Detention Act of 1950, a Cold War measure authorizing preventive detention of individuals deemed likely to engage in acts of espionage or sabotage. The 1971 law provided that "no citizen shall be imprisoned or otherwise detained except pursuant to an act of Congress." The consensus against race-based mass detentions preceded the enactment of this legislation. Moreover, the detention of Japanese Americans would have surely been approved by Congress following Pearl Harbor if such approval had been sought by the president.

Chapter 9

1. Some approaches to natural law (and its corollary natural rights) presume that there is a correct answer to every dilemma. We can discern that answer only if we can properly access the correct source: God, the Bible, the church hierarchy, the Halakah, the Shari'ah, nature, reason, a categorical imperative, a social contract—even a utilitarian calculus. Some advocates of positive law (and its corollary positive rights) also claim that positivism can provide a right answer to every legal conflict. They believe we can discern that answer as well by reference to the correct sources: the Constitution, statutes, common law, international law, treaties, and other accepted legal mandates.

2. See Alan Dershowitz, "When Torture Is the Least Evil of Terrible Options," *The Times Educational Supplement,* June 11, 2004, pp. 20–21.

3. The dispute over the right to life and choice is replicated in the arguments concerning assisted suicide, the death penalty, just war, and other deeply divisive issues growing out of the strong human impulse to "choose life," as the Bible puts it. Scientists prefer to point to the instinct to preserve one's own life and those of one's family members over the lives of strangers.

4. See "Report About English Bill of Rights," *New York Times,* October 2, 2000.

5. George Washington put it this way: "It is now no more that toleration is spoken of as if it was by the indulgence of one class of people, that another enjoyed the exercise of their inherent natural rights." Quoted in Alan Dershowitz, *The Vanishing American Jew* (Boston: Little, Brown, 1997), pp. 144–145.

6. *Troxel v. Granville,* 530 U.S. 57 (2000).

Chapter 10

1. See essays by Ernest L. Fortin in Fortin and J. Brian Benestad, *Classical Christianity and the Political Order* (Lanham, Md.: Rowman and Littlefield, 1996).

2. See, generally, Peter Gomes, *The Good Book: Reading the Bible with Mind and Heart* (San Francisco: HarperSanFrancisco, 1996).

3. According to the Internet Encyclopedia of Philosophy, "*Rule utilitarianism* is a formulation of utilitarianism which maintains that a behavioral code or rule is morally right if the consequences of adopting that rule are more favorable than unfavorable to everyone. It is contrasted with *act utilitarianism* which maintains that the morality of each action is to be determined in relation to the favorable or unfavorable consequences that emerge from that action."

4. Richard P. Feynman, *What Do YOU Care What Other People Think?* (New York: Norton, 1988), pp. 247–248.

5. See Chapter 18. Most Americans—other than Native Americans and African Americans—have been the beneficiaries of this right, since our ancestors made the decision to leave oppressive lands for this free country or to seek opportunities unavailable to them in their countries of origin.

6. Dworkin, *Taking Rights Seriously,* p. 271.

7. See Howard Gardner, *Intelligence Reframed: Multiple Intelligences for the Twenty-first Century* (New York: Basic Books, 1999), and *Frames of Mind: The Theory of Multiple Intelligences* (New York: Basic Books, 1983).

8. H. L. A. Hart, *Essays in Jurisprudence and Philosophy* (New York: Oxford University Press, 1983), p. 186.

Chapter 11

1. H. L. A. Hart, *Essays in Jurisprudence and Philosophy* (New York: Oxford University Press, 1983), p. 54.

2. Albert W. Alschuler, *Law Without Values: The Life, Work, and Legacy of Justice Holmes* (Chicago: University of Chicago Press, 2000), p. 136.

3. See Alan Dershowitz, *The Genesis of Justice* (New York: Warner, 2000), pp. 245–259

4. Numbers 35:9–34. (See, even God—or at least his translators—ends sentences with prepositions!) Recent research suggests that the urge for revenge may well have a genetic component. See Benedict Carey, "Payback Time: Why Revenge Tastes So Sweet," *New York Times* (Science Times), July 27, 2004, p. D1. Even if this is true, it does not follow that law should not try to channel it in morally proper directions, as it sought to do with regard to the biblical cities of refuge. See Alan Dershowitz, *Just Revenge* (New York: Warner, 1999).

5. I hear that cry often when I try to argue that a killer should be found guilty of manslaughter rather than murder. I will never forget a case in which my client, a woman, shot her husband and was convicted of murder. I argued on appeal that his history of abusing her warranted a reduction to manslaughter. When I finished my argument, an older woman came over to me and pulled out a picture: "This is my son

who I will never see again because of your client. She should suffer like I must." I understand why the victim's relatives are outraged at my effort to mitigate the crime that robbed them of a loved one.

6. Deuteronomy 19:6.

7. A biblical instance of "excessive" revenge is the slaughter of the entire family of Shechem in retaliation for the rape (or seduction) of Dinah.

8. My discussion of Durkheim's views concerning law and morality derives primarily from Roger Cotterrell's excellent summary in *Émile Durkheim: Law in a Moral Domain* (Stanford, Calif.: Stanford University Press, 1999). As Cotterrell notes, Durkheim "never wrote systematically about legal phenomena and his insights are scattered through many sources" (p. ix). Accordingly, Cotterrell's book—"the first detailed analysis in English of the entirety of Durkheim's legal theory" (p. x)—is an invaluable resource.

9. This would be especially so if the advocate of this universality of a particular right agreed with the general criteria for evaluating the morality of a society. See *Boston Globe,* August 22, 2001, p. A18, for a description of a "nineteenth-century custom" among certain Arctic cultures similar to the hypothetical discussed in the coming paragraphs.

10. John Rawls, *A Theory of Justice* (Cambridge, Mass.: Belknap Press, 1971), pp. 118–123.

11. Unless positive law included certain substantive institutional components; see Hart, *Essays,* pp. 49–87.

12. *Holmes–Pollock Letters,* ed. Mark De Wolfe Howe (Cambridge, Mass.: Harvard University Press, 1946), Vol. II, p. 36.

13. Jeremy Bentham, *An Introduction to the Principles and Morals and Legislation,* J. H. Burns and H. L. A. Hart, eds. (New York: Oxford University Press, 1996).

14. Cotterrell, *Émile Durkheim,* pp. ix, 17.

15. Ibid., p. 19.

16. Ibid., p. 50. This comparison may seem bizarre to those who live in societies in which religion lacks the power to enforce its commands. But Durkheim was interested less in the power of a social institution to enforce its views than in its moral authority to persuade. For the law to possess persuasive, as distinguished from coercive, authority it must embody the morality of the society. That, too, is an empirical claim, testable by sociologists, though it, too, can be transformed into a normative claim: Only laws that embody morality ought to endure. Even this is not completely satisfactory, as demonstrated by the persistence of sodomy laws (which many regard as immoral) in nations in which a majority regard sodomy as immoral and subject to government punishment.

17. Émile Durkheim and Paul Fauconnet, *Sociology and the Social Sciences* (1903; reprint 1982), quoted in Cotterrell, *Émile Durkheim,* p. 53.

18. See Dershowitz, *Genesis of Justice.*

19. Quoted in Cotterrell, *Émile Durkheim,* p. 15.

20. Cotterrell, *Émile Durkheim,* p. 57. I recognize that these philosophers actually lived in the real world, but you wouldn't necessarily know it from reading their abstract philosophies.

21. Ibid.

22. Ibid.

23. Ibid., p. 200.

24. Ibid., pp. 115–117.

25. This critical capacity is recognized very early in the Jewish religion by the story in Genesis of Abraham's argument with God over the sinners of Sodom. See Dershowitz, *Genesis of Justice*, Chapter 4.

26. Cotterrell, *Émile Durkheim*, p. 159.

27. Ibid., p. 164.

Chapter 12

1. See Ronald Dworkin, *Taking Rights Seriously* (Cambridge, Mass.: Harvard University Press, 1977).

2. See John Hart Ely, *Democracy and Distrust* (Cambridge, Mass.: Harvard University Press, 1980), p. 51; Alan Dershowitz, *America Declares Independence* (Hoboken, N.J.: Wiley, 2003), pp. 123–150.

3. Ely, *Democracy and Distrust*, p. 5.

4. Eugene Genovese, *The Slaveholders' Dilemma* (Columbia: University of South Carolina Press, 1992), p. 38.

5. Ibid., p. 47.

6. Ibid., pp. 27–29.

7. Ibid., pp. 37, 51, 53, 92.

8. M. T. Wheat, *The Progress of Americans; Collateral Proof of Slavery . . .* , 2nd ed. (Louisville, 1862), p. 19.

9. Ibid., pp. 20, 19.

10. Seth Mydans, "He's Not Hairy, He's My Brother," *New York Times,* August 12, 2001. It may become possible in the future to implant human genes into apes and vice versa. This would raise daunting moral issues.

11. Wheat, *The Progress of Americans,* p. 56.

12. Such a healthy cynicism about the honest use of selective arguments to justify a particular practice or result quickly reveals something more sinister when a respected institution, like the United States Supreme Court, is thought to be conspicuously manipulating arguments in an improper manner. This occurred when a majority of that court accepted arguments it would normally be expected to reject in order to help bring about the "election" of a favored candidate. See Alan Dershowitz, *Supreme Injustice* (New York: Oxford, 2001).

13. Quoted in Ely, *Democracy and Distrust*, p. 51.

14. *Dred Scott v. Sandford,* 60 U.S. 393 (1857).

15. *Brown v. Board of Education of Topeka,* 347 U.S. 483 (1954).

Chapter 13

1. Quoted in Albert W. Alschuler, *Law Without Values: The Life, Work, and Legacy of Justice Holmes* (Chicago: University of Chicago Press, 2000), p. 136.

2. Alschuler, *Law Without Values,* pp. 189–190.

3. In espousing this continuing advocacy approach, I do not mean to be self-referential. There are many who seek to persuade others of the long-term benefits—the utility—of a rights-based system. Many people throughout history—civil libertarians, human rights activists, and individuals with no particular affiliation—have been part of this process. I employ the first person as a heuristic device to contrast it with the views of others. My approach does not depend on the advocacy skills of any particular individual but, rather, on the collective ability of rights advocates to persuade others that the lessons of history strongly suggest that a rights-based system is preferable to a system based exclusively on power, even the power of the majority.

Chapter 14

1. Those who did not choose—Native Americans and African slaves—have also had a unique history: of victimization and oppression.

2. To add to the complexity and diversity, we are also a nation with a considerable number of authoritarians who simply follow without questioning, particularly when it comes to religion.

3. My observation that we Americans take our rights seriously does not contradict Ronald Dworkin's observation that many American and British citizens would not care if certain rights were eliminated. Nor does it necessarily conflict with Dostoyevsky's characterization of human freedom. We tend to care about our own rights, but we care far less about the rights of others, especially when they conflict with our own preferences.

4. I prefer to speak about "original assumptions" rather than "intent," since few of these assumptions were consciously or overtly thought about by the framers. There were, of course, some specific provisions of our Constitution that were not intended to be open-ended. These include the age requirements for holding office.

5. John Hart Ely's elegant theory of judicial review—justifying it as a method of clearing the channels of democracy—accounts for many, but not all, of the rights that experience shows are needed to prevent wrongs.

6. Learned Hand, *The Spirit of Liberty,* 3rd ed. (New York: Knopf, 1960), p. 190. "Liberty lives in the hearts of men and women: when it dies there, no constitution, no law, no court can save it; no constitution, no law, no court can even do much to help it. While it lies, it needs no constitution, no law, no court to save it."

7. During that terrible period in our history, courts played an important role in restraining Congress by imposing procedural restrictions on its witch hunts. See Richard M. Fried, *Nightmare in Red: The McCarthy Era in Perspective* (New York: Oxford University Press, 1990), pp. 184–188.

8. See Ely, *Democracy and Distrust* (Cambridge, Mass.: Harvard University Press, 1980).

9. For legal positivists, the amending process demonstrates that even the most basic rights—such as freedom of speech—are subject to change and that most rights

are not "unalienable." For some natural-law advocates, amending the First Amendment so as to eliminate freedom of speech would violate our natural rights. For me, I would have to persuade my fellow Americans to oppose such an amendment on the basis of our collective history and experiences with the wrongs of censorship.

10. See Amartya Sen, *Development as Freedom* (New York: Knopf, 1999).

11. A victims'-rights amendment has been introduced in Congress on several occasions, but to date it has not been enacted.

12. The Supreme Court decision in the 2000 presidential election case is a prime example of the abuse and misuse of judicial review. Invoking the "equal protection" clause of the Constitution, five Republican justices—none of whom had been sympathetic to an expansive view of that clause in previous cases—stopped the hand recount that could have changed the result of the election. In doing so, they may have indirectly influenced who will be nominated to serve as their successors on the high court, thereby eliminating an important component of our system of checks and balances. See Bruce Ackerman, "The Court Packs Itself," *The American Prospect,* February 12, 2001. This decision, which has been widely criticized by experts, neither opened the channels of democracy nor protected the rights of the disenfranchised.

Chapter 15

1. "The law" is also ambiguous. Various statutes prohibit certain kinds of abortions, but various constitutional provisions—federal and state—have been interpreted to entrench a positive-law right to choose abortion, at least under certain circumstances.

2. See *supra,* Chapter 1. See also Alan Dershowitz, *Contrary to Popular Opinion* (New York: Pharos, 1992), pp. 207–243.

3. There seems to be some evidence from some parts of the world, especially Russia, that easy abortion is sometimes used as a means of birth control.

4. For example, many believe it is moral for an army to bomb a legitimate military target even if it is completely predictable that some (but not too many) innocent civilians will be killed. So, too, it may be deemed permissible to execute many guilty murderers even if it is predictable that a small number of falsely convicted innocents will also be executed. See Dershowitz, *The Genesis of Justice* (New York: Warner, 2000), chapter 4. Some support abortion, at least under certain circumstances, on similar grounds: The intent is to help the mother, not to kill the fetus.

5. As evidence of the non-humanity of the fetus, they point to the fact that the law does not generally punish abortion as murder. Right-to-life advocates are seeking to change this.

Chapter 16

1. The 2004 documentary *Outfoxed: Rupert Murdoch's War on Journalism* helped to publicize a study that showed that viewers who received most of their news from

the Fox News Channel held misperceptions about current events far more frequently than did those who received most of their news from PBS or NPR. This PIPA/Knowledge Networks Poll, entitled "Misperceptions, the Media and the Iraq War" and issued on October 2, 2003, found that 67% of those who get most of their news from Fox have the impression that the United States has found clear evidence that Saddam Hussein was working closely with al Qaeda, while only 16% of those who received most of their news from PBS or NPR held this misperception. One-third of Fox watchers held the erroneous belief that the United States had found Iraqi weapons of mass destruction, while only 11% of the NPR and PBS audience believed this. And 35% of the Fox audience said, incorrectly, that the majority of people in the world favor the United States' war against Iraq, whereas only 5% of the PBS–NPR set held this misperception.

Chapter 18

1. In his *Discourse on the Constitution and Government of the United States,* published shortly after his death in 1850, John Calhoun wrote: "That a state, as a party to the constitutional compact, has the right to secede—acting in the same capacity in which it ratified the Constitution—cannot, with any show of reason, be denied by anyone who regards the Constitution as a compact—if a power should be inserted by the amending power, which would radically change the character of the Constitution or the nature of the system; or if the former should fail to fulfill the ends for which it was established." John C. Calhoun, *Discourse on the Constitution and Government of the United States*, vol. I of *Works of John C. Calhoun* (New York: D. Appleton, 1883), p. 301.

2. A March 28, 2004, *Seattle Times* poll found that 53% of those between the ages of 18 and 35 believe gay couples should be allowed to marry legally, while only 29% of those over age 65 approved. Susan Gilmore, "Young People Most Accepting of Gay Marriage, Poll Finds," *Seattle Times,* March 28, 2004. The University of Pennsylvania's National Annenberg Election Survey also found in a February 5–8, 2004, survey that young people were the strongest opponents of a constitutional amendment to ban same-sex marriages, while older people most strongly oppose the legalization of same-sex marriages.

Chapter 19

1. In Numbers, Chapter 20, God punishes Moses and Aaron for striking a rock in order to draw water from it, rather than talking to it as he commanded.

2. My first professional encounter with animal rights occurred in the unlikely context of a United States Supreme Court argument about the censorship of the film *I am Curious, Yellow* back in 1967. Chief Justice Warren Burger kept invoking the analogy between consensual sex and bearbaiting (despite the fact that bears do not consent to being baited). See Alan Dershowitz, *The Best Defense* (New York: Random House, 1982), pp. 165–167.

3. This is a variation of the slippery-slope argument or the pragmatic claim that we need to build fences around our core rights. More on this later.

4. Seth Mydans, "He's Not Hairy, He's My Brother," *New York Times*, August 12, 2001.

5. A similar argument is made on behalf of fetuses. When John Kerry announced that he believed life begins at conception but that he would not legislate against abortion, he was accused of creating a slippery slope that would end with legislation authorizing the killing of babies.

Chapter 20

1. Thomas Hobbes put this somewhat ironically in his *Leviathan* XVII (1651): "The laws of nature, as justice, equity, modesty, mercy and in sum, doing to others as we would be done to, of themselves, without terror of some power to cause them to be observed, are contrary to our natural passions, that carry us to partiality, pride, revenge and the like."

2. Some orthodox Jews, who generally encourage organ donation to save life, were originally opposed to corneal transplants because they only save eyesight. Many have changed their views because sight can itself save life.

3. The use of the organs of a lawfully executed person raises moral concerns, even for those who favor capital punishment. There is always the risk that in a close case, the thumb of pragmatism might be placed on the scales of justice. This would be especially worrisome if the government benefited from the use of the organs, by either selling them or directing them to favored recipients.

4. Other options could include a "futures market" for organs in which live people would agree—for a price—to donate specified organs to a "bank" that would sell them to recipients. A society might well decide that such a market was unfair or unseemly and prefer a mandatory system, or a system in which receipt of organs is conditioned on a willingness to donate them.

Conclusion

1. *The Nation*, March 15, 1971.

2. See *supra*, Chapter 5.

3. Cass R. Sunstein, "The Smallest Court in the Land," *New York Times*, July 4, 2004, p. 9.

4. See the Introduction.

5. To demonstrate the complexity of this issue, it should be noted that Justice John Paul Stevens, who generally supports a living-constitution approach, joined with Justice Scalia in this opinion, while Scalia took a much more conservative view in the Guantanamo case.

6. *Board of Regents of State Colleges v. Roth*, 408 U.S. 564, 571 (1972), quoting *National Ins. Co. v. Tidewater Co.*, 337 U.S. 582, 646 (1949) (Frankfurter dissenting). *Michael H. v. Gerald D.*, 491 U.S. 110, 138–139 (1989) (Brennan dissenting).

7. William J. Brennan Jr., speech at the Text and Teaching Symposium, George-town University, Washington, D.C. (October 12, 1985), located at http://www.politics.pomona.edu/dml/LabBrennan.htm (accessed August 26, 2004).

8. See Alan Dershowitz, *America Declares Independence* (Hoboken, N.J.: Wiley, 2003), p. 152.

9. Babylonian Talmud, Baba Mezi'a, p. 59b.

10. *Schlup v. Delo,* 513 U.S. 298, 317–318 (1995) (emphasis added).

11. *U.S. v. Virginia,* 518 U.S. 428, 441 (2000) (emphasis added).

12. Laurence Tribe, *God Save This Honorable Court* (New York: Random House, 1985), p. 45 (emphasis added).

13. *Michael H. v. Gerald D.,* 491 U.S. 110, 141 (1989).

14. Brennan, speech at the Text and Teaching Symposium.

15. This is not true of all rights. The rights to property and to bear arms tend to be favored by conservatives and disfavored by liberals.

16. Brennan, speech at the Text and Teaching Symposium.

17. Antonin Scalia, "Originalism: The Lesser Evil," 57 *University of Cincinnati Law Review* 849 (1989), at p. 855.

18. Antonin Scalia, *A Matter of Interpretation* (Princeton: Princeton University Press, 1997), pp. 3–47.

19. See Dershowitz, *The Genesis of Justice* (New York: Warner, 2000), pp. 208–209.

20. This analysis once again demonstrated the inadequacy of our current political vocabulary, in which "liberal" is often used to describe those who would conserve or expand established rights and "conservative" is used to describe those who would contract these rights when such contraction is deemed necessary to adapt the Constitution to changing wrongs.

21. See Dershowitz, *Supreme Injustice* (New York: Oxford University Press, 2001).

22. Justice William O. Douglas, who often advocated a functional or living constitution view, often cited history, tradition, and original intent when it supported the substantive outcome he favored. See his dissent to two cases in which the Supreme Court ruled against the requirement of unanimous jury verdicts. *Johnson v. Louisiana* and *Apodaca v. Oregon,* 406 U.S. at p. 380. He wrote: "With due respect to the majority, I dissent from this radical departure from American traditions. . . . The unanimous jury has been so embedded in our legal history that no one would question its constitutional position and thus there was never any need to codify it. Indeed, no criminal case dealing with a unanimous jury has ever been decided by this Court before today, largely because of this unquestioned constitutional assumption. . . . Today . . . two centuries of American history are shunted aside. . . . Until the Constitution is rewritten, we have the present one to support and construe. It has served us well. We lifetime appointees, who sit here only by happenstance, are the last who should sit as a Committee of Revision on rights as basic as those involved in the present case." (406 U.S. at pp. 381–394) Justice Marshall made similar use of historical material in his dissent in the same case: "We are asked to decide what is the nature of the 'jury' that

is guaranteed by the Sixth Amendment. I would have thought that history provided the appropriate guide. . . . But the majority has embarked on a 'functional' analysis of the jury that allows it to strip away, one by one, virtually all the characteristic features of the jury as we know it." (406 U.S. at p. 400)

23. As Justice Robert Jackson once quipped: "We are not final because we are infallible, but infallible only because we are final." Concurring opinion, *Brown v. Allen*, 344 U.S. 443 (1953), at p. 540.

24. See Dershowitz, *Supreme Injustice*, pp. 185–197, for a discussion of how relying on the courts may have weakened the right of women to choose abortion.

INDEX